INSIGHTS ON
IMPLEMENTATION

THE

LEAN
OFFICE

COLLECTED PRACTICES & CASES

Productivity *Press*

New York

Most Productivity Press books are available at quantity discounts when purchased in bulk. For more information contact our Customer Service Department (888-319-5852). Address all other inquiries to:

Productivity Press
444 Park Avenue South, 7th Floor
New York, NY 10016
United States of America
Telephone: 212-686-5900
Fax: 212-686-5411
E-mail: info@productivitypress.com

Material originally appeared in the *Lean Manufacturing Advisor*, 1999-2004.

Library of Congress Cataloging-in-Publication Date
The lean office : collected practices & cases.
    p. cm. — (Insights on implementation)
  Includes index.
  ISBN 1-56327-316-0 (alk. paper)
  1. Organizational effectiveness. 2. Industrial efficiency. 3. Office management—Cost control. 4. Industrial management—Case studies. I. Productivity Press. II. Series.

  HD58.9.L43 2005
  338'.06–dc22

                                              2004027739

08 07 06   9 8 7 6 5 4 3

Contents

Chapter 9

Part III: Taking the Right Steps

Chapter 10

Chapter 11

Chapter 12

Chapter 13

Chapter 14

Chapter 15

Chapter 16

Chapter 17

Chapter 18

Citations

Index

Introduction

Growing numbers of manufacturers are recognizing that a true lean transformation can only occur when lean principles are applied to all operations, not just the shop floor. Eliminating waste and adding value for the customer are concepts for every aspect of a business, from product design to purchasing to customer service.

In addition, companies in non-manufacturing industries increasingly grasp that they, too, can benefit from becoming lean organizations. Service businesses, governmental agencies and non-profit organizations are all jumping on the lean bandwagon, driven by a desire for the competitive advantage that can be achieved through a lean strategy.

Case studies about lean in non-manufacturing settings – office lean, as it is sometimes called – have appeared regularly in the pages of *Lean Manufacturing Advisor*, a newsletter that each month chronicles how companies are implementing lean production.[1] This collection of those articles provides you with a unique source of information. For the first time, one publication brings together a broad series of case studies of office lean implementations. These articles can provide you with insight into the benefits of applying lean to an office setting as well as the key

---

[1] For more information regarding the articles in this book, including the original dates of publication, please refer to the citations section.

challenges and pitfalls, the critical success factors and the most useful tools.

Books that teach you the concepts and techniques of lean are important. This collection provides a valuable supplement to those types of books by describing the real-world experiences of office lean implementers. We hope that you will benefit from these experiences of others as you progress forward on your lean journey.

Part I

Focusing on the Customer

OVERVIEW

Since creating value for the customer is a fundamental principle of lean production, it is critical to understand who your customer is and what your customer considers valuable. The articles in this section highlight companies with a particularly sharp focus on that issue.

And since lean principles are typically thought of in connection with manufacturing, it takes a special vision to see how they can be applied to non-manufacturing areas. Therefore, we begin this section with a chapter describing Toyota's recognition that sales and marketing can be made lean. A key part of Toyota's plan to achieve that goal is working closely with distributors to identify how to best serve customers.

Fujitsu is another company with a solid vision of what it can become through a lean transformation. The core of its effort, described in Chapter 2, is to shift from "make-and-sell" to "sense-and-respond" – meaning sensing and responding to customer needs and desires.

Improving the voice of the customer in its product is also the goal of Timberline Software, whom we profile in Chapter 3. By revamping its processes for designing software and forming multi-functional teams to discuss all issues, Timberline has achieved significant gains in time-to-market, quality and cost.

In a call center, customer service representatives hear the voice of the customer every day – but the programmers who develop the call center software may not. By having its programmers come to the call center, watch the representatives and listen to the calls, LG&E Energy streamlined its processes, improved its technology and improved customer satisfaction. Read about the company in Chapter 4.

And in Chapter 5, we describe efforts to respond to customers when they can be at their most demanding – in a restaurant. The owner of the Sweet & Savory bakery and café believes that lean holds the key to growing his business, and is running his business accordingly.

These businesses all understand that providing maximum value and eliminating everything not considered valuable is essential to achieving success and competitive advantage – and that a clear definition of value is the foundation for that strategy.

These chapters provide useful examples of how always keeping the customer in mind gives you a clear focus on the heart of your business.

1

New Toyota Center Seeking to Make Sales and Marketing Lean

August, 2002

Toyota has launched a long-term, global effort to apply the principles of lean manufacturing to sales and marketing.

In April 2002, Toyota opened the Global Knowledge Center in Torrance, Calif., an organization responsible for helping the company's sales and marketing arms around the world apply its principles to their operations. The Center is part of the University of Toyota (see sidebar below).

"The Toyota Way in manufacturing is the Toyota Production System," says Tony Fujita, a Toyota vice president and the man in

charge of the new Center. "This is our attempt to create a Toyota Way in sales and marketing. We can become efficient. We can eliminate the waste that may exist. We can apply the concept of continuous improvement to how we sell and market our products and how we take care of our customers."

Tony Fujita, Toyota

As an example, Fujita notes that he visited Toyota distributors in Europe, the United Kingdom and the Middle East. "Each distribu-

The University of Toyota

Based in Torrance, Calif., the University of Toyota is an organization designed to provide training and skills development to a wide range of Toyota associates worldwide.

The newly launched Global Knowledge Center is one of four University branches. The three others are:

- College of Associate Education & Development. This branch encompasses six centers that focus on, respectively, Strengths Management, Automotive Business Operations, Leadership Development, Personal & Professional Development, Financial Services and The Toyota Way.
- Dealer Education. Within this branch are the School of Product and Technical Education, and the School of Retail Professional Development.
- Learning Technology Group, which focuses on selecting and implementing technologies to fit Toyota's educational philosophy. It also guides e-learning programs from a technology perspective, and provides consulting on process redesign and change management.

tor was planning their own model launch, in many cases the same model throughout the world," he observes. "If we can find a collaborative approach to launch a product globally, that would be a huge elimination of waste."

Continuous improvement is one of two pillars that Fujita says the Center is built on, the other being "the respect for the individuals and the respect for the relationships that we have throughout the world."

Initially, Fujita and his staff of eight will be pursuing what he describes as a four-stage process of development:

- First, they will work to build communication and relationships with distributors worldwide. "We really don't have any kind of a dialogue or relationship with distributors," he notes. The effort will seek to "establish a consensus globally on the

Toyota Way in sales and marketing."

- Second, "we will try and establish a mechanism to share best practices in how we go about selling cars, and in how we maintain contacts with customers."

- Third "to establish some sort of global performance measurement, to compare notes with each other." Likely metrics include market share, customer loyalty and satisfaction, and profitability of the dealership organization globally.

- The fourth stage is comparable to General Electric's use of so-called "black belts" in Six Sigma to train others within their organization. "We want to take the expertise and knowledge that exists throughout the world," Fujita says. "For those countries that need some help — in the used car business, for example — we can send a black belt, say to far eastern countries. Thailand, for example, doesn't have a used car business."

While a clear time frame has not yet been established, Fujita says his organization will be developing a three-year business plan. He also suggests that work during the first two years of the Center's operations will focus on the first two stages of the plan.

"The ultimate goal is, of course, to sell additional cars and become the most successful and respected car company, not only the U.S. but in every corner of the world. That's a long-term perspective," Fujita states. The work of the Center is intended to support achieving Toyota's goal of 15 percent global market share by the early 2010s.

He notes that some of the challenges his organization faces include geographic distance, different languages and different cultures.

Fujita stresses that within Toyota, customers are ranked first, followed by dealers and then manufacturing. He comments, "We don't want to take the approach that we are the experts and have all the knowledge. We see ourselves as a group that has no authority, but must prove our worth by showing value.

"As we complete visits to various distributors, we see very proud and very talented resources throughout the world. They are very proud of their association with Toyota. That's a tremendous asset to begin with. It's tremendously exciting to talk to the Toyota people all over the world. We're having a great time right now."

TAKEAWAYS

- Communication with distributors is the foundation of Toyota's efforts.
- Sharing best practices and establishing metrics are essential.
- Using experts to provide support is necessary to sustain such an effort.

2

Transforming a Service Firm

June, 2003

As head of European strategy and operational development for IT services giant Fujitsu, Steve Parry has set an ambitious goal for his company.

What he wants is simple: To reach the point where, in his words, "Fujitsu is to service what Toyota is to manufacturing."

Parry wants not only the success and recognition achieved by Toyota. He seeks to transform Fujitsu — a $37.5 billion company with 170,000 employees in 65 countries — into the same kind of flexible, customer-focused, value-adding enterprise that Toyota is.

In other words, he wants Fujitsu to become lean.

This transformation effort was launched several years ago in Europe and is slowly spreading through Fujitsu operations around the globe. As much or more than anything else, it involves changing the way the company's people think — moving from "make-and-sell" to "sense-and-respond," as Parry puts it. It involves changing traditional ways of doing business, creating new approaches to serving customers and restructuring contracts between Fujitsu and those customers.

It is based on the firm conviction of Parry and others that lean principles are the path to the greatest success for a services firm, as surely as they are for a manufacturer.

Organisational Transformation: Old to New

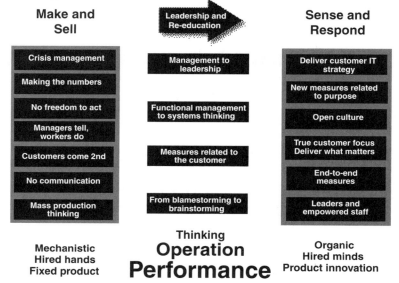

Make and Sell	Leadership and Re-education →	Sense and Respond
Crisis management	Management to leadership	Deliver customer IT strategy
Making the numbers		New measures related to purpose
No freedom to act	Functional management to systems thinking	Open culture
Managers tell, workers do		True customer focus Deliver what matters
Customers come 2nd	Measures related to the customer	
No communication		End-to-end measures
Mass production thinking	From blamestorming to brainstorming	Leaders and empowered staff

Mechanistic
Hired hands
Fixed product

Thinking
Operation
Performance

Organic
Hired minds
Product innovation

How effective is your end-to-end organisation?
Value to Failure ratio - working on the mix

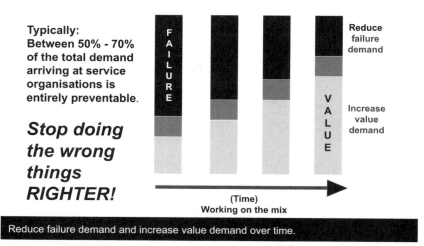

Typically:
Between 50% - 70%
of the total demand
arriving at service
organisations is
entirely preventable.

Stop doing
the wrong
things
RIGHTER!

FAILURE

VALUE

Reduce
failure
demand

Increase
value
demand

(Time)
Working on the mix

Reduce failure demand and increase value demand over time.

Fujitsu's new approach is described in these slides from a presentation Steve Parry gives to both managers and potential clients.

8

Benefits of a New Approach

Fujitsu announced that, for the 2002-2003 fiscal year, its London-based services division was profitable for the first time in five years.

The division earned an operating profit before exceptional items of £59.6 million and a pre-tax profit of £30.5 million.

Richard Christou, CEO stated that "Contract performance has improved and productivity has increased significantly." A company news release said actions to improve performance during the past year included creating a new management team, selling non-core businesses and "improving our financial discipline."

The effort is already achieving benefits. "By delivering what matters to the customer, contractual levels have improved," he states.

A New Paradigm

Services are only one source of business for Fujitsu, which is known for a wide range of computer hardware products — from notebook and desktop computers to servers, from storage systems to ATMs and retail point-of-sale units.

The company offers a variety of IT outsourcing services, including maintenance of IT infrastructure and operation of technical support help desks.

Parry joined the company in 1999, with a background that included experience in the automotive industry and a familiarity with lean principles.

At that time, he says, some people within Fujitsu recognized that the mass production-like approach that was then being used to deliver services was not the way to go. "They wanted to develop IT services that were able to transform client IT environments," Parry recalls. "But while the concept was there, they didn't know by what method to do that."

Fujitsu at the time was "a very fragmented company," says Parry,

The Subtleties of Change

The greatest obstacle to promoting a new approach within Fujitsu, Steve Parry found, was that "I was talking to people that were very well-educated in the old mindset."

As a result, he developed a PowerPoint presentation that lays out in detail the values and approaches of the "sense-and-respond" model and how it differs from "make-and-sell."

That presentation is also designed for Fujitsu customers. That's because what Fujitsu provides in services can "look very similar to jobs done by our competition. It's difficult to say we think differently and do things differently. The customer will say 'yeah, right.' I had to give the customer some models. The only way to communicate this stuff was to contrast the two models in operation."

The word "lean" does not appear anywhere in the presentation. "The problem with 'lean' is that it has some connotations," Parry explains. "It's unfortunate, but it's true. People associate lean with manufacturing, and what most people have as a concept of manufacturing is a lot of people in a factory producing things. That gives the wrong image of what we are doing in our services organization."

While most lean experts say that top management support is critical for an initiative, the approach at Fujitsu has been different. Parry launched his effort and pilot initiatives with backing from his immediate superiors, but without involvement from the very highest levels of the huge Fujitsu hierarchy.

"Six months ago, we were finalists in the U.K. national business awards for customer focus," Parry recalls. "The first thing the CEO knew about this was that he had to give a press conference (about the awards). He said, 'what's this stuff going on?' Then he said, 'that's great, you just carry on doing that.' If we had gone to him in the first place, and talked about subjecting the whole organization to this, he'd have said 'no way.'"

who is based in London. For example, IT infrastructure maintenance was handled by one department, and help desks were handled by another, even when one client was using both types of services. Parry's approach: "Why don't we design an end-to-end organization of which the help desk is just one component?"

However, changing Fujitsu's approach to services involved more than just linking departments together. It involved an entirely different mindset about the services being provided.

Many of the principles he promotes are fundamental lean concepts (though Parry generally does not use the word lean — see sidebar page 10). For example, he talks about designing against customer demand, rather than according to functional specialization; placing decision-making authority on the front line rather than with a manager; establishing measures related to customer purpose, rather than to budgets, targets and standards; and basing the client relationship on delivering what matters, rather than on arbitrary terms in a contract.

A New Way of Helping

Help desks, or call centers, are a prime example of where the new principles are being applied. A typical call to a help desk might be someone complaining that they are unable to make a printer work. Traditionally, the call is logged, and information about all calls might be used to identify the mean time between fixes, or which printers generate the greatest number of calls.

Also, the traditional approach might emphasize keeping calls short and helping the client fix the problem on the first try. The contract for the service often provides that the client is charged based on the number of calls made, and may guarantee that a certain percentage of problems will be fixed on the first call.

But Parry sees a number of problems with the traditional approach. The help desk may succeed in providing the required percentage of first-time fixes, but "there's no incentive to improve the infrastructure" so that the problem stops recurring, he notes. In addition, keeping calls short — minimizing what is called "handle time" — shouldn't be the ultimate goal, he suggests: "Why should we try to reduce the average handle time on work we shouldn't even be doing? The average handle time on work going up is seen as good, provided demand is going down."

11

("Demand" in this case refers to the client's need for services; a user calling to say "I can't print" is demand. Therefore, the goal is to reduce that demand.)

The new approach requires restructuring the contract with the client, so that the client is charged for each user of services — regardless of whether any particular user makes one call to the help desk, 10 calls or 100 calls. "The only way that works is to take waste out of this," Parry explains. "The incentive to us is to remove demand."

(In a presentation he gives to both managers and potential clients about the "sense-and-respond" approach, Parry states: "Typically, between 50 percent and 70 percent of the total demand arriving at service organizations is entirely preventable.")

Another part of the new approach is to map the value chain "to measure the different types of demand," Parry notes. "We don't track the solution, we track the problem.

"We say demand is 'I can't print.' So if a customer says 'I can't print,' what is the whole end-to-end response to all 'I can't print' problems? We know because we measure it statistically, with statistical process controls. The mean time is maybe 50 hours, plus or minus 10 hours. That's what our control chart says. That's a long time and a lot of variation. We look at the special causes in that variation. We find out which types of printers cause the most pain. We might map that as a sub-demand.

"What's the worst experience that a customer has? Fifty hours is a pretty bad experience. Incidentally, most of the functional goals say everything is fine, but the user experience is 50 hours. And the guy who ends up creating value for the customer by fixing it is really way down the line, and all preceding steps create no value."

Addressing this type of problem involves providing incentives to help desk workers "to remove the failure demand." It might also involve providing the front-line workers with greater training so they can solve the problem without passing it on to someone else.

Then, "if we do have to pass it on, the guy (who then gets the call) is getting a genuine good call because we have taken some of the low-level work off high-level guys, and they are able to do more higher-level stuff."

That last point, Parry boasts, has led to a reduction in turnover among engineers and help desk staff from 42 percent to 8 percent in two years.

Another example of the new way of thinking Parry describes concerns software Fujitsu has created that, he says, "is able to predict what part of IT is likely to be failing soon. The software can put in patches and work-arounds so the client doesn't feel any degradation in service." The result is that the system works, and everyone assumes there is no problem, when in fact the original programming is deficient. A better approach would be to take information from the software to identify how the design of the original program could be improved. "We don't want to do a work-around. We need to design those out," says Parry. "We should improve the IT environment and not stick plaster over it each time."

Providing Value

In his presentation, Parry refers to the airline bmi, a Fujitsu client, as an example of the new approach. While Fujitsu is providing the airline with IT services, he notes "It's not about IT, it's about flying aircraft... it's about the flying passenger... it's about creating business value." Fujitsu's goal for its client is "to keep bmi passengers flying through the provision of an effective, efficient IT infrastructure."

A list of 10 targeted improvements for the client includes several that don't even mention IT:

- reduced queues at ticket office.

- reduced queues at check in.

- boarding delays reduced.

In another example, Parry talks about a large Fujitsu client (whom he did not identify). In this case, the client — a large company — decided to divide its outsourcing business among several providers. Fujitsu was given a contract for help desk services only.

"We applied the same principles anyway," Parry states. "We were able to demonstrate how well — or not — other companies were performing. We said to the client, you need to talk to one of your suppliers over here. He accounts for 30 percent of the chase calls coming into the organization. If he improves, service improves to your users. Demand calls dropped 24 percent in one month. The client has seen an awful lot of intelligence about third parties, even though we only had the low end, the help desk, but we were providing high-end intelligence." Eventually, Fujitsu won contracts for all of the client's outsourcing business.

A Global Journey

Parry says that the new approach has achieved a "70 percent penetration" of all Fujitsu operations in Europe. He has recently introduced the concepts to offices in Australia and South Africa.

And in an ironic development, he has also taken the concepts to Japan — the home of the Toyota Production System.

"If you look at manufacturing in Japan, they've understood for a long time, but services in Japan haven't moved that much at all," says Parry. "One of the major questions I had from the Japanese guys was, 'we're not sure if it will fit our culture in Japan. Can you convince me?' I had a wry smile on my face."

TAKEAWAYS

- A services transformation involves a cultural shift from "make and sell" to "sense and respond."
- Contracts with clients must be restructured to support lean approaches.
- Different metrics are required for service operations, such as call centers.

Revamping Design Process Increases Speed and Quality

November, 2003

To a manufacturer, designing and developing software might seem like a strange business.

When a manufacturer produces a product thousands of times, it must repeat its production and assembly processes for that product each time. In contrast, a software developer goes through its production processes once; the finished product is then simply reproduced, perhaps by being copied on to a CD-ROM.

However, the processes for developing software — and the issues that arise in those processes — are, in a broad sense, similar to those of manufacturing. For example, the processes may not be fully focused on creating value for the customer. They may contain waste. The software company faces the same kinds of competitive, time-to-market issues as the manufacturer.

In short, the process of creating software can be improved by applying the principles of lean production.

That, in fact, is what is happening at a small number of technology companies. They are reaping big benefits as a result.

At Timberline Software, "our overall estimation is that we improved time to market, quality and costs upwards of 25 percent in each of those areas," says Ammon Cookson, who was a program manager at

Planning the Process is Critical

The key to lean software development is to begin with a series of abstractions that define what the development is all about, according to Jim Sutton of Lockheed Martin. Sutton is an experienced IT professional and co-author of a forthcoming book on lean software development.

Sutton believes that the development should begin with what he calls value resolution. "If you think of software as 'I'm going to write a program,' then you are really doomed from the beginning," he declares. "You have to look at the characteristics of the world you're putting your system into and the changes that you want your system to make to that world."

For example, he explains, if you are designing software to change the speed of an airplane, you need to know the current speed, the engine parameters, the attitude and altitude, and "then you come up with what you are going to do — I'm going to rev up the engine, or it may be that I'll just point the nose down."

The key characteristics become the basis for software requirements and an architecture for the software. The next key step is to identify what is known as a domain design, a set of related systems.

For example, Sutton says, "aircraft are related systems. They do different things. Some go very fast, some are low and slow and carry lots of stuff. But they are doing similar things, from a functional

Timberline when it first embarked on a lean journey.

The transformation of Timberline, an Irvine, Calif., company that produces financial and operations software for the construction and real estate industries, did not come easily. "Software engineers will tell you that software is not like manufacturing and you can't apply manufacturing techniques," Cookson recalls. "'We're not building widgets.' I could go through the whole list of things that come up with software development. There was quite a bit of resistance to it initially."

As with manufacturing, the creation of a lean software company requires a new way of thinking. Employees and managers in all areas must develop a new, shared focus on the customer and fol-

standpoint and from an information standpoint. In those cases, you tend to be dealing with similar kinds of databases.

"If you can identify a domain, a set of similar systems, and you can identify what it is about the domain that stays constant from system to system, from one version of a system to the next version, if you then base your architecture on those things, what happens is you make those the heart of the structure."

That architecture can then be used to support different but related systems, like different aircraft, with few modifications.

"The most important two principles are understanding the customer requirements and understanding what is the changeability of the different elements in the domain," Sutton states.

In actual development, he adds, "when you choose your methods, tools, languages, you make all those decisions with the goal in mind of making it as easy to verify and quick to verify the software as you possibly can." For example, you might not choose UML (unified modeling language), opting for some other language instead.

Sutton believes one of the problems with software development today is the capability maturity model (CMM), a set of criteria developed by Carnegie Mellon University for judging software producers. These criteria, which have been adopted by segments of the federal government and other institutions, "drive people toward choosing mass production techniques, not lean production techniques and technologies," he says.

low processes that help identify customer needs. Every step in a process must be identified and measured — in ways never done before — and steps may be eliminated or rearranged.

The Voice of the Customer

Amy Flaxel, who holds the position of director for the office of continuous improvement at Timberline, notes that the company embraced lean principles to improve quality, improve time to market and "improve the voice of the customer in the product."

In addition, she says, "we had grown to the point where processes had become non-standard, even non-documented. Knowledge was confined to people's heads."

Timberline hired Crow Development, a consulting consortium that helped provide training and direction for the software company. (Cookson still works for Timberline, but has also joined with some of the Crow consultants to form a new consulting firm, Lean 360.)

Part of the process of convincing people that lean principles could be applied to software development, Flaxel says, was to help them all gain a common language using the terms of lean production. That "provided a really good foundation for continuous improvement, but also predictability," she states.

Timberline began its lean journey with a pilot project headed by Cookson on development of software to help customers implement databases. And the first step in that project, he says, was to create a software product concept — a definition of "what the customer experience is going to be" and an identification of customer needs and requirements. Potential features in the software to be created were identified as either necessary or attractive, and were then weighted and scored.

Using a cross-functional team to evaluate features was critical, Cookson states.

He explains: "In traditional software development, an engineer may come to you and say 'I can produce this piece of functionality the customer will value, and do it in one or two or three ways, and each one doesn't take any more time. Which one do you want?' You take that from the perspective of quality assurance, and the question is which one is easier to test? Now with a whole concept, you bring sales in and look at that feature, and it's which implementation is easier to sell? Marketing may say, 'which one is easier to present?' The whole concept or goal of that front end is to take a cross-functional team, so each individual coming out of there understands much better what's going on with the customer. While it doesn't necessarily tie directly to some of the lean manufacturing principles most people are used to, it's one of those areas I think it's important to highlight because as the team is moving forward into actual production, it needs to really understand the customer."

Development of the software product concept is followed by a planning or "orchestration" phase in which the concept is transformed into a production plan. "Think of it like a mountain," says Cookson. "We're going to disassemble it piece by piece, break it down into smaller and smaller units, define what the units are, define an order in which they should go through the value chain and assemble them at the back end."

As an example, he suggests that a given program may need to include a calculator as part of the software. This is likely to require at least three units of work: creation of the business rules that actually manipulate the numbers in the desired ways, creation of the user interface that allows the user to operate the calculator, and possibly another system below the business rules that enables the calculator to store values.

Identifying Units

However, turning a sequence of units into a practical production plan requires a good deal more work.

One necessary step is calculating takt time, Cookson notes, though takt time at a software company is not the same as at a manufacturer. Takt time is normally defined as the amount of time available to produce a product based on demand, calculated by dividing the production time available by the number of products ordered.

In software, explains Cookson, the time available is the amount of time between the start of work and the deadline when the software must be delivered. For example, with tax accounting software, the product must be complete in time for the next tax season. The time available is then divided by the number of units of work that are necessary to complete the product. This determines the time available for each unit of work — the software version of takt time.

One of the requirements built into the Timberline pilot project was that no task could be longer than five days.

Once units are identified, they must be sequenced properly to optimize production. And to track progress, every person involved in the work was required to use a time stamp to note the beginning and end of each unit. That requirement caused a "huge kickback initially," Cookson admits, but adds that "what the teams realized in the end was this was a method to help them understand how the system is actually working."

Another significant change from traditional development methods was that quality assurance would test each unit as it was finished — just-in-time testing — rather than waiting to test the entire program after its completion. Cookson notes that this essentially eliminated what is called the stabilization phase in software development, an often-lengthy testing period at the end of the process. Flaxel adds that the end product was of significantly higher quality, which benefits the customer and "results in a huge savings once we get out to the customer and the customer is no longer finding defects."

The result, Cookson says, is that "what we delivered was exactly what the customer wanted," rather than the typical scenario where a customer provides feedback on version 1.0 to get what they really want in version 2.0.

Timberline has been applying lean principles to other parts of its operations, most recently order processing. Flaxel says the company has been able to reduce by 99 percent the time it takes to process orders for its consulting services, simply by removing waste from the process, including unnecessary hand-offs and review cycles.

Both she and Cookson stress that senior management support and employee involvement are critical factors to the success of any lean initiative.

Flaxel adds that when applying lean principles to a non-manufacturing operation, it is important to do "whatever kind of work you can do to help smooth that translation and to really take the time to customize the education to your particular audience."

TAKEAWAYS

- Many lean principles apply as well to software design as to other processes.
- Cross-functional teams, common definitions and segmentation of work are particularly important.
- A version of takt time should be calculated, and new approaches to quality testing are required.

4

Call Center's Transformation Produces Award for Service

October, 2002

In March of 2002, J.D. Power and Associates reported that Kentucky-based LG&E Energy received higher satisfaction ratings from its small business customers than any other utility company in the nation.

According to Molly Sutherland, who headed the company's Business Service Center, LG&E won that honor at least partly by applying lean principles to service operations.

Before the Business Service Center was launched in the spring of 2000, representatives were answering only 20 percent of calls within 30 seconds. Their record improved to 96 percent two years later.

"The primary focus of the first six months was just to reduce muda (waste)," Sutherland says, "including the distance from where you were working to a fax machine, streamlining technology, getting the technology so you could answer the phone and walk around at the same time. We set up a system so that everybody knew what was in everything. Cabinets were coded by color. It was very, very unsophisticated. We had a kanban system. We kept things very minimal — that reduced clutter and waste as well."

Work was also standardized, with clearly mapped-out procedures for everything from re-reading a meter to putting a contract together. Computer programs were also standardized, in the order in which information appears on a screen, for example. "I had programmers spend a half hour in the call center listening to customers and watching reps on the screen," Sutherland says.

Sutherland, who described her experience at a University of Kentucky conference in early 2002, is a staunch advocate of the idea that the benefits of a lean transformation can be achieved in an office or service setting just as well as in a manufacturing plant. She stresses that achieving improvements requires a total commitment to lean concepts.

"The best thing is to fully understand the principles," she explains. "Don't make them into a program of the month. Walk the talk, and weave it into every single day's behavior."

Strategy Shift

Before the current system was established, LG&E had what Sutherland calls a "cost-ineffective" system. Telephone service representatives were not specifically focused on serving business clients. Costly field representatives handled much of the contact with businesses.

"We made a decision to move away from the face-to-face sell strategy," Sutherland notes, shifting to a multi-channel effort with significant telephone contact (though the company still can dispatch representatives to the field when necessary). A separate Business Service Center was carved out of the consumer call center. Sutherland was told in March of 2000 that the center had to be operational 45 days later.

Prior to that time, LG&E appeared to be providing good service. The company's service to small business customers has been ranked by J.D. Power as the best in the Midwest for three consecutive years.

(LG&E's residential service operations are also rated well by J.D. Power in a separate survey, apparently without the application of lean principles.)

But Sutherland believed that lean production would make a difference at LG&E. That belief came from her experience working with the utility company's industrial customers, encouraging their efforts to become more efficient. "If a plant was really efficient, then its growth and expansion would happen in Kentucky, and that would sell more electricity," she observes.

The shift in service strategy and the lean transformation have had an impact. The Business Service Center has a staff of 10, which is 52 fewer people than with the system of field representatives. The 10 representatives were originally organized to handle up to 400 calls per day; they now cope with up to 650 calls per day.

Technology has also helped. "In the past, we would have people physically located in central Kentucky. It's very rural. If they need to contact a new client, they would write up a contract, take it out there and have it signed," says Sutherland. "We made the contract electronic. We filled the blanks and emailed it. We accepted electronic signatures. We did it for both the convenience of the client and us. It saved tons of money and time.

"If the customer wants to see a bill, we email the bill. We talk about the document together. Nobody had to wait on appointments. It's a different way of doing business for us."

As with any lean effort, motivating employees is important. Sutherland says her philosophy is "Have fun. Celebrate successes. My group loves to eat, so we bring in food."

She also occasionally has had staffers tour the facilities of customers in the field. "They got out of the office. For a call center environment, that's huge," she notes.

Conversely, internal meetings are not attended just by service representatives. "I have linemen come to meetings. I have meter readers. I have billing people," says Sutherland.

New Challenges

Sutherland left the Business Service Center in early 2002 after being asked to lead IT projects for LG&E. She says that lean principles have not spread much beyond the Business Service Center, at least partly because many people have been focused on recent acquisitions.

But she also says she is attempting to apply lean techniques to her current work. And she approaches that effort with enthusiasm.

"The more you know (about lean), the more you understand and appreciate — and to me, the more fun and interesting things are," she says.

TAKEAWAYS

- Eliminating waste through changes in office layout and in technology can accomplish a great deal.
- Standardization of work with clearly mapped procedures is essential.
- Establishing contact between service workers and other departments, as well as with customers, supports improvement.

New Restaurant Owner Sees His Future in a Lean Lunch

April, 2004

Rob Shapiro intends to use the principles of lean production — a focus on the customer, flow, continuous improvement, the right metrics — to serve lunch.

Actually, lots of lunches. Shapiro and his wife, Dayna, were scheduled in March, 2004 to take ownership of Sweet & Savory, a bakery and café in Wilmington, N.C. They believe that by adhering to a lean philosophy, they can profitably manage and expand this small business, even though it is not a traditional manufacturer.

"Lean is a business system. It's not a manufacturing system," Shapiro declares. "It's one where the tools can be used in almost any business. Lean can be used in food service."

In fact, Shapiro views lean as not just a set of tools. Lean principles are at the very heart of his business plan, which projects that the bakery's business will more than double over the next three years.

He also believes that lean concepts are not entirely new to the food service industry. "You go into any restaurant, they have visual management. They have seating charts, tickets. Already, the principles are being applied, although I don't think anybody really called it lean."

Opportunity for Growth

This unfolding story of a lean restaurant results from the convergence of two other stories.

One is the evolution of Shapiro, who has degrees in industrial systems engineering and management, into a lean advocate. That was largely the result of 11 and a half years spent at Alcoa, working with the Alcoa Business System in the company's Kawneer division. That experience ended in December 2002 when the company sold the division. Shapiro and others accepted a buyout package.

He then spent four and a half months with a company in Chicago in a job "that ended up being a mismatch," Shapiro recalls. He and his wife, who has a background in finance and marketing, then reviewed their situation; "we had talked in theory about running our own business," he notes. "We were ready for something different." Shapiro, who is 36, says the two of them believed "we were young enough to make some mistakes, but old enough not to make too many."

The other story is that of the restaurant itself, founded (about a dozen years ago) and run by David Herring, a chef. Sweet & Savory's sole location is about a mile from the North Carolina shore, and the restaurant employs 15 people. Shapiro says its annual sales are about $770,000, with about $400,000 of that from a café that only serves lunch. The remaining revenues are divided about equally between sales from a bakery and from a wholesale and catering business. Profit is about $100,000 per year.

The restaurant's growth over the years has been the result of "pure word of mouth," Shapiro says, adding that Herring spent only about $1,100 a year on advertising and did not use signs to promote the business.

"There's enormous potential," Shapiro believes. Herring — whom he describes as "a chef, not a business guy" — is selling, he adds, because "he wants something different, and it's getting beyond his business skills." Under the sale agreement, Herring will stay for a transitional period of three months, with the possibility of continuing on if everyone gets along well.

Strengthening the Culture

Shapiro praises Herring for having the "proper management style" and for developing a company culture with "large elements of trust — he has the staff close for the day, or open for the day. He lets the rest of the staff handle money."

Shapiro's goal now is to build on that culture. "We really start by focusing on the business needs, with any activity or spending going toward meeting customer needs." He identifies those as, first, cleanliness, health and safety; second, food quality and consistency; third, good service, and fourth, good atmosphere.

From there, he intends to encourage a culture where "it's about fixing things, it's not about finding fault. That really comes from our leadership in the organization, not blaming people for systemic problems. Also, creating a culture where people aren't rewarded for heroic actions, they're rewarded for operating within the system."

Part of that, he adds, is to "create a culture where we fix problems as they come up. Utilizing lean thinking, it's really about teaching people to ask for help, and don't wait until the customer is affected. We teach people that there is a reason a recipe is there, and if they know they have to deviate from it, they have a problem. You don't not melt cheese in the broiler to get the order out — you ask for help."

Similarly, "we might have a slot for 20 orders being prepared at one time. If you end up with the 21st order, somebody has got to ask for help. We'll have built-in signals, built around queue size."

Shapiro's approach will also include focusing on flow: "We want to make sure there is no confusion. Orders are cooked on a first-in, first-out basis, and prepared properly. The workers flow fairly well right now, with the way things are laid out."

He also plans "a single measurement — it might be the number of meals served." And he plans to stress "a binary connection, with the customer, with the supplier. We'll focus on really looking at pull. How do we improve upon that process, within our inventory management, instead of randomly ordering? We're having a fair amount of waste, five to 10 percent. Maybe we can cut that in half."

Many tools of lean production can be applied, such as standardized work, Shapiro states: "We'll be highly defining the work of one person, such as how long it takes to make a sandwich."

And even the concept of takt time — the time available to produce a product, based on demand — can be applied, he says: "You know the rate at which customers are coming in the door, the average rate. Say I want to be able to feed 200 people in two hours. How do I do that? If I improve signage, and I believe I can increase that to 250, can I drop my cycle time to meet that increase?"

Growth Targets

Shapiro's plans are ambitious. He hopes to expand the wholesale operation, adding staples. He plans to open for breakfast (and eventually, perhaps dinner as well) and open on Sundays. He plans to go after more catering business, and go after more tourist business, which he says Herring "really hasn't done at all."

In his business plan, "without even factoring in dinner, there's a fairly easy potential to go to $1.7 million, $1.8 million a year over a three-year period," he contends.

And beyond increasing revenues, he hopes to cut costs as well while continuing to take care of the workers. He says, "Our cost of goods sold is about 33 percent of sales. That probably should be 26 to 28 percent. That swing is worth $35,000 to $50,000 a year. That's enough to cover at least a very basic health plan."

TAKEAWAYS

- Lean principles can be applied to food service as well as any other industry.
- A lean strategy can form the heart of a business plan.
- A focus on meeting customer needs is critical.

Part II

Improving Flow

OVERVIEW

On the shop floor, parts and raw materials flow through manufacturing and assembly processes as they become finished products.

But the concept of flow applies to everything else in business as well. The chapters in this section address issues of flow in non-manufacturing situations. Building designers, project supervisors, billing managers and postal workers are the players in these stories. Their experiences can help you identify and address issues of flow within your enterprise, no matter what type of product or information is flowing.

In Chapter 6, invoices are flowing, rather than parts or materials. This chapter describes the experience of the city-operated ambulance service in Phoenix, Arizona, which bills citizens for ambulance services, generating invoices for up to 60,000 emergency calls a year. Through application of lean principles to the invoicing process, the city is able to produce most invoices within 24 hours after the call.

Building designs may be a bit more complicated than invoices. All features of the planned structure must be presented accurately, and customer preferences – as to color, for example – must be recorded. FBi Buildings, the focus of Chapter 7, found that by applying a variety of lean methods, including a reorganization of its design department, the company handles more business with fewer people and fewer mistakes.

Flow is particularly important with a high-volume operation. Canada Post, the Canadian postal service, handles several million pieces of mail every day. Chapter 8 describes how, through lean initiatives, the organization now processes more mail each day but has less inventory – mail on hand – at any given time.

During construction of a building, flow is extremely complex, with a variety of contractors and tradesman performing different tasks, each with their own materials arriving at the same site, trying not to get in each other's way while avoiding downtime. Chapter 9 profiles the efforts of a small, but growing number of construction companies who are finding that a lean approach to construction gets the work done in less time at lower cost.

6

Ambulance Office Responds to Calls for Improvements

November, 2002

Saving a life takes a lot of paperwork.

That's true, at least, for the ambulance service operated by the fire department in the city of Phoenix. Aside from administering whatever medical treatment is necessary at the scene, the paramedics have to obtain the name, address and insurance information of the victim. Back at the office, that has to be translated into an invoice. (Like many cities, Phoenix bills citizens for ambulance services.) Connections must be made with Medicare, Medicaid or a private insurance company.

In a city of roughly 1.5 million people, this process is repeated many times over. The department handles up to 60,000 emergency calls a year, sometimes as many as 250 a day. That adds up to a lot of invoices.

And that is why, for 15 years, the department has applied the techniques and tools of lean production to processing all that paperwork. The result is a well-oiled office machine. Many invoices are processed within 24 hours. Collections are high enough that revenues exceed the costs of emergency ambulance service. It's a showcase example of how lean principles are just as applicable to an office as they are to a factory floor.

"The manufacturing model is not mutually exclusive of public service," says Collin DeWitt, a leader of the transformation of the Phoenix operation. Processing the paperwork, he explains, "is just like building an end product. The outcome was a billable invoice for services."

A Monopoly Operation

Phoenix got into the business of providing emergency medical services in 1985. Before then, seven private ambulance companies served the 450-square-mile city. With the old system, according to a history on the city's website, "average response times were unacceptable, approaching 20 minutes — and a standard of a 10-minute response time was met only 50 percent of the time."

The city fire department competed in — and won — a bidding process to provide ambulance services, implementing its system in November 1985. DeWitt became the fire department's deputy chief for medical services.

At that time, in the mid-to-late 1980s, he was taking graduate courses at Arizona State University. He studied concepts of continuous improvement and quality management under Dr. William Fechter, a lean and Six Sigma expert with extensive experience as a university instructor and a consultant.

DeWitt was concerned that a governmental operation might not embrace improvement and quality concepts. "When you've got a monopoly, it becomes easy to become very inattentive to both internal and external customers," he says. "The bigger government tends to do that. If we don't have what you want, it's your responsibility to find it, not ours. What we do isn't always sufficient either. If we don't have enough, we just increase taxes. It has nothing to do with making the customer feel they're getting a bang for the buck."

However, in winning the contract for the ambulance services contract, the fire department clearly had a mandate to improve upon past operations. Almost from the outset, it was able to do that, in part due to factors that had nothing to do with lean manufacturing.

For one thing, each of the private companies served only part of the city, and each tried to focus on more affluent areas so as to maximize collections and profits. The fire department, with 50 fire engines, a dozen ladder trucks and 25 ambulances, serves the entire city.

In addition, "we had career personnel," DeWitt notes, in contrast to the workers in the private companies, who tended to be "transient... young people looking for what they wanted to do in life. They (the private companies) were paying very low wages. There was no retirement process. The public safety retirement system is a very well-funded system. Salaries are adequate. There is a career path. The package lent itself to a much better delivery system."

However, it wasn't just providing emergency medical services that was new to the fire department. For the first time, the department was issuing invoices. The state of Arizona requires that citizens be billed for ambulance services — and it sets the rates cities can charge. Therefore, if a city wants its ambulance service to be self-supporting — as Phoenix does — it must make sure that its costs for the service do not exceed the effective limits on revenue created by the state rates.

In addition, the department wanted to make sure that both the delivery of service and the billing went smoothly because "once people start paying for something, they expect a certain level of performance. Expectations increase significantly. We had to raise the bar on service delivery and how it was delivered, simply because there was a revenue stream attached to it. It took a bit to get everybody on board," DeWitt explains.

Same Ideas, Different Product

Generating invoices is very much like manufacturing products, DeWitt believes. Improving that process means applying lean principles in much the same way as would occur in a factory.

"Response forms went through a very close review and addition of information in an office of about 13 customer service reps," he states. "They went through all the documentation and added something at each stage. I liken it to a production line. We interposed quality control at varying spots. If a billing form comes to the front end, we do a quick scan to make sure we have all the signatures, the address. It goes to research. There's another station that does nothing but Medicare, another nothing but Medicaid. It's just like building an end product." Most bills are received by consumers within 48 hours.

Process improvements were not just a one-time thing. Continuous improvement was the guiding principle, with constant measurement, evaluation and feedback part of the operation.

Incentives were important, DeWitt stresses, since rescue personnel "didn't like asking who is the insurance carrier, who will pay, who do we send the bill to. We had to put something in there that drove and recognized their efforts. Employee recognition had its birthplace in the fire department."

Employees who delivered quality work were given a gold pin, and "that became sought after in the organization," he adds. "We would school them on what they need to do — accurate information, if it was readable. We got down to penmanship, for heaven's sake. A lot of things fed into a successful process."

The city's website proudly describes what has been achieved: "The direct cost for emergency ambulance service is presently about $7.7 million per year. Cash receipts total over $12 million. The collection rate of adjusted accounts receivable experiences an average of 71 percent — well within the 60 percent required by contract."

The Right Attitude

Those figures are actually DeWitt's legacy, since he retired from Phoenix three years ago to become chief of the fire department in Gilbert, Ariz. — which does not provide municipal ambulance service.

He offers this advice to others in the service field: "The idea of continuous improvement is forever. That notion, no matter what you call it, has to be part of your organization's culture. The applications we do on a daily basis are making widgets and a product that is pleasing to the consumer. We just have different terms for it. What makes manufacturing successful also bleeds over to customer service — which is what we're all about."

TAKEAWAYS

- Constant measurement and evaluation of performance are just as important in office operations as in manufacturing.
- Quality control at a variety of points must be part of the processes.
- Employee recognition is important in motivating workers.

7

Whether Office or Factory, the Same Principles Apply

October 2003

In applying the principles of lean production, Joe Ely doesn't see any difference between manufacturing products and designing buildings.

Consider his description of what the design process used to be like at FBi Buildings, a Remington, Ind., company where he is director of quality:

"The symptoms basically were excessive costs and uncontrolled overhead expenses, particularly on the drawing side. There were inaccuracies. The attitude was 'I know it's not right. I know I'm making mistakes, but I need to do something, so I'll do it.' That's entirely equivalent in the manufacturing world to 'I know my machine is out of calibration, but I'm going to make quota anyway, so I'll make more bad parts.'"

Ely's attitude enabled him to spend three years improving the design process at his company. The result: "When we started this whole process in September of 2000, we had 11 people in our design group. We are now [in 2003] doing 20 percent more business with eight people. That's a productivity assessment. We had turnover of 50 percent per year. Now we're changing less than one person per year. That's an assessment of quality of life, or stress. Mistakes are at one-third of the level they were."

Ely spoke in October, 2003, at Productivity's 8th Annual Lean Management and TPM Conference and Exposition in Nashville. He described how FBi Buildings has applied lean principles in its purchasing group to improve practices in its supply chain. That effort was the second major focus of the company's lean journey, after the improvements in the design process.

But in both cases, Ely emphasizes, "what we found is that the core principles of lean apply fully in an office setting."

Improving Flow

A major portion of FBi's business comes from the design and construction of commercial post-frame buildings — simple, economical structures with wooden frames and sheet metal walls.

All the buildings are designed and built the same way, but each one is unique, made to a particular customer's specifications.

Those specifications are initially recorded by a salesman in the field, then communicated to the DTO — Design/Take Off — Group. The DTO staff must translate the customer's desires into actual drawings and building plans.

But problems can arise when information is unclear or incomplete, or when it contains discrepancies. For example, colors might not be specified, the location of a door might not be clear, or a sketch might show four windows while the contract calls for five.

To help bring about improvements, the company worked with Hal Macomber, an independent consultant.

A number of ways were found to improve the process. For example, workers created a sales aid — a general purpose three-dimensional drawing of a building on which specific details could be easily written.

However, the biggest focus was on improving flow within the DTO Group, where multiple people were giving multiple requests to multiple workers.

"There was just a general sense of chaos or a lack of control," Ely recalls. "There was a lot of activity, and nothing was coming out. A cardiologist calls that fibrillation."

One source of delays was that, when a DTO employee ran into a problem, he would typically just put the project aside and work on something else.

To address these kinds of issues, and to work toward the lean goal of single-piece flow, management issued a declaration in 2000 that each DTO staff member could only have one job on his desk at a time.

And to make sure each job could be completed, management instructed employees to use what was called a Line Stop system — stop work and call for help to solve any problems.

In a manufacturing operation, this process might involve an employee pulling a cord to light up an andon board. At FBi Buildings, employees were given whistles.

"It's a loud, audible alarm," smiles Ely. "Then we assigned people who, when they hear the whistle, within 60 seconds show up at a guy's desk, and then we solved the problem. They did not leave until it was solved."

From Pool to Cells

After instituting this new flow system, no further changes were implemented for the next six to eight months while employees got used to operating the new way. "It was such a massive cultural change for us, it was about all they could absorb at once," Ely states.

The next step to drive flow "was to reset how we determined who was going to do a job and when," he notes. Previously, a scheduler assigned projects to the staff, but Ely realized that work "wasn't adding any value." A physical queue of jobs was created, consisting of simple hanging file racks that indicated priority and time for completion. Staffers simply took projects out of that queue.

Job flow before Kaizen #2

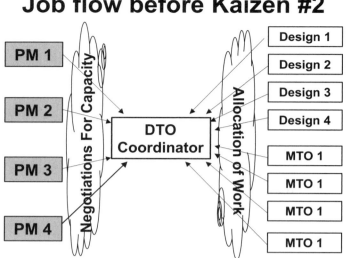

"Pool" Concept, with a Scheduler

Job flow after Kaizen #2

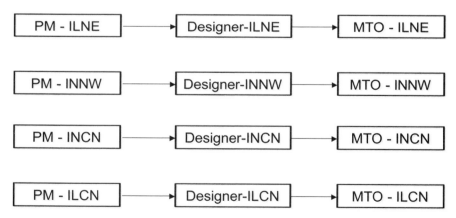

At FBi Buildings, a DTO (Design/Take Off) Coordinator used to allocate work from each project manager (PM) among designers and MTO (material take off) workers. The coordinator position was eliminated and teams pull work from a queue of hanging files. Each team consists of a project manager, designer and MTO worker. The teams are identified by the geographic areas they serve: Illinois NE (ILNE), Indiana NW (INNW), Indiana Central (INCN) and Illinois Central (ILCN).

The scheduling position was eliminated, and that employee was transferred to another job.

At the same time, the company moved from a "pool" arrangement to work cells. The scheduler had been assigning work to employees in a pool, receiving projects from project managers and distributing them among designers and material take off (MTO) employees. After the change, specific teams were created to simplify the flow of work, each team with a project manager, designer and MTO person (see diagram opposite). Ely says this dramatically improved accountability and job satisfaction, shortened cycle times and decreased error rates.

While the cultural change at FBi Buildings was difficult — a consultant used early on became a "lightning rod" for employee complaints, Ely says — that change is now complete, he believes.

Today, "the most outstanding ideas come from the workplace," he says, adding that relentless efforts to eliminate waste are now second nature.

Ely states, "We have found these things are sustainable. It really surprised us, especially some of our veterans. We're three years into it, and they're like, whoa, it's not a flavor of the month. It clearly gains momentum."

TAKEAWAYS

- Workers cannot be receiving requests from multiple persons for flow to work.
- Problems must be addressed as soon as they are discovered.
- Assignment of jobs through a pull system using a physical queue is better than having a person act as scheduler.

8

Neither Culture Nor Equipment Stops Postal Transformation

October, 2003

Canada Post, the Canadian postal service, was an organization that had operated a certain way for decades.

Following World War II, it was staffed largely by former army personnel who used what was essentially a "command-and-control" form of management, according to Rochelle Duhaime, general manager of process excellence. Not surprisingly, the 55,000-employee organization developed a history of militant labor relations, Duhaime says.

In addition, she notes that many of Canada Post's long-time managers were trained on batch production and on "the more machines, the better."

This was not an atmosphere conducive to lean production.

But that was then, meaning prior to 1996, when the organization's leaders decided lean was the way to go. The lean journey they began has been slow and difficult, but it has also been productive.

Today, Canada Post processes more mail in less time using less space. And perhaps an even greater accomplishment is that its corporate culture is changing.

Improving flow with cells like this one enable Canada Post to process more mail in less time with less space.

"We're not over the hump yet, but we're in much better shape," says Tom Charlton, senior vice president for operations. "We're much better aligned. Many more managers understand what we're talking about. It's all dramatically different from where we were in the early 90s. If you brought a manager from the early 90s into our operation now, it would be total culture shock."

Charlton, who described the Canada Post experience at the 2003 19th Annual AME Conference in Toronto, notes that "we were converting managers and employees who had grown up in a specific world. There is no other industry in Canada like it. We couldn't learn from anyone else. We had a set of specific difficulties we had to overcome that were unique in some sense to Canada Post and the postal industry. There was a certain culture built up over many, many years. All those things we had to overcome. It was not a magic formula. We had to work our way through this."

Physical Transformation

In 1996, "we sort of hit a wall" in production and processing, Charlton recalls. "We were looking for another way to get the job done, both culturally and physically. We had implemented some projects in Toronto and Montreal, and dashes of lean were used as part of the projects."

About that time, Charlton and a colleague heard a presentation by lean expert and author James Womack. "We became convinced this was a strategy that had some potential," he states.

Canada Post did some work with Womack's Lean Enterprise Institute, but didn't use outside consultants to a great extent. "We tried to build slowly internally," Charlton says. "It was self-education, group learning."

The organization designed its own 5S training materials. That was partly because it needed both English and French versions, and partly because "we wanted to make it applicable to a postal operation," Charlton notes. "We had slightly different contexts, and we wanted to make it so our people could understand it in terminology we were using in our world."

Physical changes were made, including many that might be classified as right-sizing equipment.

"We moved equipment closer together and put in place conveyers and mechanisms to shorten transportation. We have small, simple conveyer systems. We replaced some of the very large, overhead and in-ceiling parcel sorters. We took out almost all of the old parcel sorters from the 70s and eliminated a lot of forklifts," says Charlton. "We've got close to one-piece flow in parcel operations. In letter operations, small batch is about as far as we are able to go."

The results have been significant.

"The amount of time a piece of mail is actually being transported or physically moved around is down to about a third of what it was before," Duhaime boasts. Specifically, Charlton notes that a piece of mail might have taken 24 hours to move through a facility before the changes and now takes about eight. He concedes that those eight hours might include only 17 seconds of value-adding work, but stresses that recipients of mail are still getting better service.

Another measure is work in process. Canada Post used to have 11 to 12 million pieces of mail being handled at any given time; today, the figure is down to about six million.

And a great deal of space has been freed up. Entire floors have been closed in some locations, and some cities that previously had two facilities are now down to only one. However, there have been no layoffs, Charlton says; workers have been reassigned, and the workforce has been reduced through attrition.

Building Buy-In

However, perhaps the biggest change is in converting the corporate culture. "We took the track of doing the physical things, changing the look of the place, cleaning it up, and having the cultural things build behind the physical changes," explains Charlton.

Duhaime says one technique that helped get employees involved was a mockup of a proposed new layout, put together with building blocks that could be moved around. The mockup was placed in the middle of a shop floor. Associates were drawn to it and helped move the blocks around to help find the best design.

"This was one of the first programs where we were allowed to grow with the program," she notes. "Employees were allowed to get behind it, and make mistakes. That went a long way to make people more relaxed."

Charlton adds that "the whole issue around work groups — with the union, to get them to accept that kind of a structure took a long time."

The biggest achievements, he says, are "the whole understanding of our management team around continuous flow, one-piece flow vs. batch processing. The whole idea of improving the workplace in terms of how your staff behaves."

For the future, Canada Post is starting to implement a system of managing plants by value stream, rather than management by shift manager, and "the other big thing we still have to get to is organizing all work in cells, load balancing the operation. We're still not very good at that," Charlton adds.

He concludes, "I guess we all didn't expect it to be quite as tough as it was. It was three steps forward, two steps back. We always made progress. It was a long, difficult road. This is not an overnight thing."

TAKEAWAYS

- Right-sizing equipment, as well as placing machines closer together, significantly improves flow.
- For certain types of small items, small batches may be the closest you can get to one-piece flow.
- Physical improvements and mock-ups can help achieve cultural change.

Builders Seek to Demolish Inefficiency

December, 2002

In the typical construction project, "all the research shows workers are standing idle 20 to 30 percent of the time," says Gregory Howell, co-founder and COO of the Lean Construction Institute.

At the same time, huge piles of materials often sit at construction sites untouched for weeks because they cannot be installed until certain parts of the job are completed — and they arrive before that happens.

Chuck Greco, CEO of Linbeck Construction, Houston, adds that on the typical project, the rate of completion — meaning parts of the job being finished by the time the contractor said they would be finished — is usually only around 40 percent.

Why so much waste? "What you had on a project typically was a superintendent who would give orders, informing people about the general contractor — 'here's what we're going to do this week, everybody follow us,'" explains Paul Reiser, vice president of production and innovation for Boldt Construction, Appleton, Wis. "There was a lot of fragmentation, subcontractors doing their work with a lot of disregard for the work of others."

Howell agrees: "The problem that many people see in construction is litigation. But the reason litigation arises is because I've contracted my activity, you've contracted another activity, and our

Boldt Construction officials say they improved jobsite production and achieved other benefits by applying lean principles to construction of this $182 million Cardiac Center project for St. Lukes Medical Center in Milwaukee Wis.

efforts to optimize our own parts put us at odds with one another."

All this is beginning to change. A small but growing movement — spearheaded by organizations like the Institute and companies like Linbeck and Boldt — is applying the principles of lean manufacturing to construction. With new approaches to scheduling designed to make construction work flow through a pull system, contractors and their customers are starting to see dramatic results.

"It's not uncommon for our best lean projects to be characterized by 20 percent schedule improvement, significant cost savings and highly satisfied customers," says Reiser.

While there have been efforts in the past to address construction inefficiencies, he adds, they typically focused on the productivity of individual tasks rather than the overall effort. The result: "You can pour concrete really fast, but you don't necessarily get the job done faster."

Applying lean principles to construction really means applying them to project management. This transformation may not utilize manufacturing cells or quick changeovers, but it does involve mapping the construction processes, determining the most efficient flow of work and establishing a pull system.

Leading Edge Efforts

The lean construction movement goes back to at least 1993, when the International Group for Lean Construction (IGLC) was founded. Much of that group's focus is outside the United States; "In some ways, the U.S. (construction) industry is not particularly a leading industry," observes Howell.

Howell co-founded the Lean Construction Institute in Ketchum, Idaho, in 1997 with Dr. Glenn Ballard, who was also a founding member of the IGLC. Both men also do consulting work separate from the Institute.

Another arm of the movement is at the University of California at Berkeley, where Ballard and Prof. Iris Tommelein, both within the university's Construction Engineering and Management Program, teach a pair of courses on lean construction. Tommelein maintains the mailing list for the IGLC.

The stated mission of Howell's Institute is "to extend to the construction industry the lean production revolution started in manufacturing." So far, Howell says, the movement has only reached a small segment of U.S. builders, commenting, "we're flying under the radar of the industry."

Tommelein agrees that lean in the construction industry is still in early stages, with a fairly low level of awareness among builders, though she adds that "a lot of people say they know what it is."

She stresses that "what we're talking about is very radical, the same as it was in the manufacturing industry, where the notion of reducing setup times, for example, was quite radical, compared to the long-held belief that setup times were a given. It's certainly a para-

Lean is the Right Formula for Rice Chemistry Building

At the beginning of 1998, Linbeck Construction was hired to renovate an 83,000-square-foot chemistry building at Rice University. Work on the building was scheduled to take 14 months.

But that was before a number of top executives of Linbeck and Rice attended a lean conference. The executives became convinced that lean was the way to go, and were also impressed by a conference speaker who said that in order for a project to work, you need a crisis.

So they created one: A Rice executive told senior project manager Kathy Jones that the job had to be done in 11 months.

After reviewing plans and deciding to negotiate with the major subcontractors to pursue a lean approach, she says, "I went back to my boss and said, 'I'm willing to attempt it if you are.' We took a hard look at the schedule. We all bought in that we could do it in 11 months."

The project included its share of challenges. For one thing, the building dated back to 1925. Most new buildings have 15 or 16 feet between floors, but this site had only 13 — and only 10 in the basement.

In addition, the original schedule assumed that the architect would supply complete drawings at the start of the project. But as things turned out, only the basement drawings were supplied at first, followed by the first-floor drawings a month later, and other floors after that.

"We went through rocky waters in the beginning," she relates. "It was all so new to us, foremen having to put schedules on paper and having to commit to what their manpower was. We developed a pull schedule. We started with the end date and worked backwards by defining major milestones."

In early stages, weekly completion rates were only about 50 percent. "But toward the end of the project, we were hitting in the high 80s," Jones boasts.

She describes the effort: "When these foremen were developing their work plans, they had to do a six-week lookahead, and a weekly plan. The six-week was more general, such as put in sheet metal on

digm shift, a different way of thinking that has many implications."

But construction is an industry that nearly everyone agrees operates inefficiently and can achieve significant benefits by becoming lean.

the first floor. On the weekly, it got very detailed — hang the pin feed of duct work in room X, with how many men, how many hours it would take. They had to compare with major milestones to make sure they were still on track.

"We made sure that if there was a problem, we could identify it immediately. They have to tell us why they didn't meet items they had described in their weekly work plan. We kept track of what the major hiccups were. If we started to see trends, we could call the project managers and say 'get some guys to help your guys.' We tried to find the source of the problem."

In developing the initial schedules, at first "the plumber and the sheet metal guy were butting heads" because each wanted to do his work first, Jones notes. But because the plumber had to install considerable amounts of the glass pipe used in a chemistry building, "we kept trying to tell the plumber, you don't want welding sparks hitting your pipe."

The foremen were able to schedule delivery of materials better, with the plumbing foreman doing the best job, Jones says, explaining that normally he liked to deliver a year's worth of pipe up front, letting it sit at the job. With this project, he never shipped in more than a week and a half's worth of materials. And whereas he often hired a tractor-trailer to take away leftover pipe at the end of a job, in this case he required only part of the space in a pickup truck.

Once the subcontractors understood the benefits of lean, says Jones, "we had the backing of their companies to do it the lean way. They found out they made more money and it cost them less. And because we communicated with each other, there was very little rework."

"We did not extend our schedule," Jones relates. "We actually built it up in nine months, and got moved in in January (1999) on schedule. We were able to do it under budget, and at the end of the day, all the subcontractors were still friends. Everybody communicated a lot better. Everybody got to be really good friends. It helped build trust and respect that I think is uncommon for a construction job."

And today? "I wouldn't do it any other way," Jones says.

Linbeck, for example, saw substantial gains in a lean pilot project at Rice University four years ago (see sidebar above).

At Boldt, Reiser offers several examples:

BOLDT

Six Week Lookahead — Constraints Analysis

Project: Healthcare

Boldt Schedule Contact: e-mail: / Phone: / Fax:

X = Repeated Items

Week of 05/14/01

Repeat	Activity	Responsible Party	5/14	5/21	5/28	6/4	6/11	6/18	Safety	Contracts / C.O.'s	Submittals/Eng	RFI's	Materials	Labor	Equipment	Prerequisite Work	Space	Explanation of Constraints	Action Required By:
	BASE BUILDING																		
X	Expedite stone production	BDI	X	X								X						Exterior stone was ordered 3/19/01; Expect on site early 5/28.	Dan J.
	Brick Work	BDI	X	X	X	X	X										X	We need to wash brick for review on 5/30/01 & possibly re-do So. In-fill wall after that.	Dan J.
X	Roofing - curbs	Langer		X															
	Curtainwall installation	Klein Dickert			X	X	X										X	Need north wall brick first	Joe B.
	Cut new duct openings in existing roof/ 3rd floor	Boldt / Illing			X							X						RFI #18 - Verify locations	Richard S.
	Install Louvers	Boldt/Illing			X	X												Boldt will install arch. Louvers; Illingworth will install HVAC louvers.	Richard S.
	Relocate CCTV and power lines thru new penthouse	Pieper		X	X	X	X										X	Need to coordinate w/security. PH walls needs to be rocked first	John W.
	NEW ORTHO OR'S 23 AND 24																		
	Structural support in ceilings	Duwe	X	X	X							X					X	Review owner cut sheets for lights and med gas booms	Dan J.
	Stainless Steel Top Lead-time	Streich				X	X											Ordered 4/6/02; 8 wk lead-time	
	Doors, Hardware Lead time	BHHM	X	X														Doors will be delivered to Service Painting's shop; shipping 5/1/01	Becky K.
	Stud framing	Davco			X	X	X	X									X	Need to relocate duct & elec. Line before W wall can go up	Becky K.
	MEP demo	Pieper/Illing	X	X														Schedule elect. Shut-downs w/Steve N. & Brad (CVPAR)	John W
	MEP rough-in's	Pieper/Illing		X	X														
	Drywall	Davco				X	X	X											
	Owner Equipment on Site	SLMC					X											Steris cabinets 20012 will be on site 5/22/01. Cabinets 2011 will be on site 5/30/01	Robert D.
	SDS INTERIOR RENOVATIONS/ BUILD-OUT																		
X	Fabricate Phase 2 (Existing SDS) Millwork	Precision	X	X	X														
	Phase 3 (New Areas & Cherry Panels) Millwork Shop Drawings	Precision			X	X					X							Boldt will hold dimensions for cherry panel walls so we can order this material.	Jeff J.
	Lead time on ICU's/ auto operator	Besam			X	X	X											8 week lead time; ordered 4/2/01	Dan B.
	...ient room 3847 and 3849	Boldt		X	X	X									X			Turn over to owner by 6/18/01	...rren M.
	...nt room 3866	Bol...		X	X										X			...over to owner by 6/18/0...	...n M.
	...26E for Elec...				X													...needs this room to... ...area; Demo hard... 6/6/0...	
					X														

BOLDT

Weekly Work Plan

Project: Healthcare

Boldt Schedule Contact: / e-mail: / Phone: / Fax:

X = Repeated Items

Week of 5/14/01

Repeat	Assignment Description — Remember the Five Criteria for Release of Assignments — Specific, Sound, Sequenced, Sized, Safe	Responsible Party	Make Ready Needs — Work that Must and Can Be Performed Prior to Release of this Assignment	M	T	W	T	F	Comments
	BASE BUILDING								
X	Wash brick @ 2nd floor	Rick J.	Will review w/ Brad, David on 5/16/01	x					
X	Roofing - curbs	Joe B.		x	x	x	x		
	Curtainwall installation - E. Elevation Framing	Joe B.					x	x	
	Curtainwall glazers prep North elevation	Richard S.			x	x			
	Cut new duct openings in existing roof/ 3rd floor	Duwe	3rd floor will be cut on Saturday				x	x	
	Install Louvers	Bud T.	Price from Duwe			x	x	x	
	Install angle in Gamma Knife ceiling			x	x	x	x	x	
	NEW ORTHO OR'S 23 AND 24								
	Review structural support in ceilings	Robert D.	Need clg. Lay-outs	x	x				
	Stud framing	Darren M.			x	x			
	MEP demo	Joe B.			x	x	x	x	
	MEP rough-in's	Jeff J.					x	x	
	SDS INTERIOR RENOVATIONS/ BUILD-OUT								
X	Fabricate Phase 2 (Existing SDS) Millwork	Jeff J.		x	x	x			
	Release order on ICU's/ auto operator	Jeff J.				x	x	x	
	Issue drwg. For isolation room doors	Jeff J.					x	x	
	Tape walls on patient room 3847 and 3849	Jay G.		x	x	x	x	x	
	Install door frame - Patient room 3866	Darren M.	Due on site Wednesday	x	x	x	x	x	
	Demo hard ceiling in toilet room	Darren M.							
	S...T-DOWN'S REQUIRE...								
X	...n shut-down	Jorda...							
	...t-down: East ...	M...		x					
	Lines ...		Need ...				...s has o...	
	......		......						

Boldt Construction uses the Last Planner production control system from the Lean Construction Institute, which involves creation of a Six Week Lookahead schedule (top) and a more detailed Weekly Work Plan (bottom).

- The company completed a $14 million correctional facility in Wisconsin four months earlier than originally planned, a 22 percent improvement over traditional project delivery.

- A $12 million college fieldhouse was finished six months early, "at 20 percent less cost than our competition had on a nearby similar project three years earlier — at a high level of quality and architectural finish," he says.

"Last year we compared concrete productivity on lean projects versus non-lean projects," Reiser notes. "The results indicated a 25 percent improvement in concrete productivity. The improvement may not be completely attributed to lean, but we do recognize that eager adopters of lean on our construction projects also tend to be innovative thinkers when it comes to operations design. When you combine lean production with innovative operations design, the result is highly reliable and productive project delivery."

Greco says that Linbeck has long been dedicated to efficient operations, with a process called TeamBuild. He sees lean as "the catalyst we could insert in our TeamBuild system as a science, and really gain the optimum from what our corporate knowledge had been building on." Linbeck is gradually implementing lean processes and expects to be using them in all projects by next year. Greco says lean projects typically achieve 80 to 90 percent completion rates.

Benefits, he adds, include greater reliability in meeting schedules and containing overhead costs; during the design, being able to "capture and incorporate into the design a lot of value;" and a lower capital investment cost for the building owner.

Howell adds, "We see numbers in the range of a 10 to 30 percent reduction in cost and time. We believe we are seeing data that shows improved safety. The 'hair on fire' index goes way down — people rushing around like their hair is on fire."

Planning and Pull

One key to making the construction process lean is creation of a pull system. Managers begin by looking at what the completed project should be, then work backwards, identifying each preceding step. Later processes determine what earlier ones will be, and when they should take place. That's critical, says Howell, because "you can't do things just in time if you don't know what time it is. You have to get the work flow under control, and that happens only in planning."

Linbeck and Boldt both use an Institute system called Last Planner for production control. The system involves both a six-week "Lookahead" schedule and a weekly work plan.

According to the Institute, front-end planning belongs in the project definition and design phases. That planning produces master schedules, which "are expressed at the level of milestones, typically by phase," according to the Institute. "Phase schedules feed into lookahead windows, usually 3 to 12 weeks in duration."

These processes make scheduled tasks ready for assignment; the tasks are placed in Workable Backlog. Weekly work plans are formed by selection of tasks from Workable Backlog.

On the job site, teams review progress weekly, identifying whether all scheduled tasks have been completed and the reasons why any weren't. Action is taken on root causes to prevent future problems.

"It forces people to get together once a week for an hour and do collaborative planning," says Reiser. "They make commitments to each other based on pull. When we meet the next week, we track the reliability of our planning, how many of those commitments did we actually meet — the plan percent complete.

"One of the biggest benefits is a much higher level of communication and awareness. It becomes a highly collaborative process. There's a new feeling of communication and participation for the people that are actually doing the work. We've empowered people on the job sites to make decisions."

Everyone agrees that once subcontractors become a part of the process, they give it their full support because they also benefit when projects are completed earlier at lower cost. Greco says building owners are typically supportive as well, but he notes that designers may offer resistance because "many architects are not really production-oriented."

A Lean Expansion

As contractors gain experience applying lean principles to actual construction, they gradually seek to extend the lean transformation.

"Because of the success we've had at the job site production level, we're trying to drive lean further into the design phase," explains Reiser. "Traditional project delivery is fragmented. Design takes place in a design office and the drawings are thrown over the wall, so to speak, to the contractor. We say it shouldn't have been designed this way, and we throw the contracts back over the wall."

He also notes that at Boldt, "we are mapping our job support processes including job setup, cost forecasting, payroll, accounts payable, purchasing, tool and material handling, and more. Value stream mapping these processes has revealed 30 percent to 60 percent waste in specific areas."

Similar actions are being taken at Walbridge Aldinger, a Detroit construction firm that began a lean initiative in 2000, but [as of 2002] hasn't yet applied the principles to projects. Employees are being trained in lean and internal operations are being streamlined, including invoicing, equipment storage and more, according to Remo Mastroianni, quality director.

Overall, the movement has a long way to go. As Greco observes, "You've got to have persistence to do this. This is not a natural thing for our industry, using flow charts and setting up the value and doing things other than straight implementation. We're not only training our organization, but training the industry. It's not an easy thing to do."

TAKEAWAYS

- Applying lean principles to construction projects can cut the time needed for a project by 20 percent and save money.
- Contractors and subcontractors must plan together, with all following the same agreed-upon schedule.
- Planning must be based on a pull system, working backwards from what the completed project should be.

Part III

Taking the Right Steps

OVERVIEW

Where do you begin with an office lean initiative? And which lean methods and tools will produce the greatest benefits when applied to an office setting?

Since lean principles have traditionally seen the greatest application in manufacturing, managers who work elsewhere often fail to see how they are applicable elsewhere. Far fewer resources exist to provide guidance in adapting lean tools and methods for use off the shop floor.

The chapters in this section can help you address these common concerns. Whether you are wondering how to run a kaizen event, what data you need to measure performance, how to create visual controls or how to build buy-in and momentum, the experiences of the companies highlighted here can be of assistance.

Chapter 10 kicks off this section with some simple but worthwhile advice about applying 5S techniques and visual controls to an office setting. The "gold standard" described here is worth remembering. Chapter 11 then offers more advice about applying 5S, but in an uncommon way: to a computer hard drive.

The importance of building workforce buy-in to a lean transformation cannot be underestimated. Early successes can help generate momentum, as executives at Siemens Business Services were quick to learn. Their experience, including the benefits they achieved, is described in Chapter 12.

Kaizen events are a lean tool not just for the shop floor. Chapter 13 profiles Bundy North America, a company that dramatically shortened the time it takes to offer business quotes to customers through application of so-called white-collar kaizens.

Kaizen events can also work wonders when applied to invoicing and receiving processes, as described in Chapter 14. This first-person account details the kaizen schedule and the key areas of waste targeted, as well as the reductions achieved in the numbers of process steps.

Perhaps the greatest gains occur when improvement efforts are part of a company-wide strategy covering all areas, both manufacturing and non-manufacturing. Chapter 15 describes Delphi's efforts to broaden its lean approach and deploy just such a strategy.

Rockwell Collins applied a variety of lean methods and tools in its efforts to improve the process of producing technical manuals. From the design of cells and the use of visual controls to broader issues, such as change management and the definition of value, their efforts – detailed in Chapter 16 – can serve as a model for other organizations.

A more quantitative approach to identifying and targeting waste in non-manufacturing operations is described in Chapter 17. A spreadsheet program developed at Delphi transforms data about operations into reports that clearly identify value-adding and non-value-adding operations, and bring into focus the greatest opportunities for improvement.

And in Chapter 18, we detail how North Jersey Media has gone beyond basic implementation of lean methods. The publisher has linked lean principles to daily decision-making, as a means of sustaining the changes and making lean thinking an integral part of how the company operates.

First Steps to Making Your Office Lean

By
Charles Skinner

March, 2003

Why should I bother applying lean principles to my office when I can easily find anything I need right away?

You don't need to — if you are the only person who uses the office and the information and materials in it. However, if anyone else needs to access the information and materials in your office then the question needs to be asked, "How long will it take anyone to find what they need in your office?" The gold standard is that anyone should be able to find anything they need in their own office in less than 30 seconds. And anyone else should know the who, what, when, where, why and how in any office, even if no one else is there, in less than five minutes.

How do I begin?

The first step in the procedure is 5S: Sort, Set in Order, Shine, Standardize, Sustain.

Sort — Identify what is needed and what is not needed to get your job done right now. Anything that is not needed is set aside in a Red Tag area, which is a safe area for holding (not throwing away) things that you are not sure you need. Empty the Red Tag area routinely, but only after you have allowed enough time to know with certainty that what is discarded is not needed.

Set in Order — A place for everything and everything in its place. This is a tricky step. The key is to put things where it is easiest to replace them. In any workplace people get busy. When we are busy we put things where it is easiest to put them. If the right place is difficult to use, we will put things in the wrong place, and everything will get out of place.

Shine — Clean, but do more. Use cleaning as a form of inspection to find the source of contamination and eliminate it.

Standardize — Determine the standard procedure that you and others will use to maintain the first three Ss. This includes random inspections for at least 30 days until people get in the habit of doing things right.

Sustain — This takes education, training and changing habits. Generally speaking you must follow the new standard procedures for at least 21 days in a row to develop a new habit.

I, and others in my office, have done a pretty good job with the first four Ss, but we are having a very hard time with Sustain. What should we do?

Sustain is indeed the most difficult step. If we cannot Sustain, the work we do in the first four Ss can be a waste. There are three things to focus on to help with Sustain.

Visual Display — Label to make it perfectly clear where things belong and what the procedures are. Labels are not generally for the people who work in an area, but for others who are new to the area, or for those might need to know things about the area.

Visual Metrics — Effective communication of instructions, directions, and standardized work in the form of documentation, on paper or in computers, makes work easier and more successful. Communications that are ambiguous, inaccurate or incomplete can lead to major problems getting work timely and right. Up to 60 percent of the problems that occur in the work environment are created by problems with communication.

Visual Controls — There is a tendency to think that because one control has been put in place, we have done all that needs to be done to keep things controlled. In fact, there are many choices when trying to control what has been put in place. There are six levels of Visual Controls:

Level 1: Share information

Level 2: Share standards

Level 3: Build the standards into the workplace

Level 4: Use alarms

Level 5: Stop defects

Level 6: Eliminate defects

The lower levels are quick to install and very low-cost but may not be as effective as you need. Higher levels are more complex and expensive, but give much greater control. The top three levels are also known as Mistake Proofing.

TAKEAWAYS

- Applying the steps of 5S is a good way to begin a lean office initiative.
- Establishing visual displays, metrics and controls are essential to sustaining improvements.
- The standard is to be able to find anything in your own office in 30 seconds, and in someone else's office in five minutes.

11

5S Techniques Can Clean Up the Hard Drive of a Computer

May, 2003

The stages of 5S — sort, set in order, shine, standardize and sustain — can be modified and applied to the electronic files of a computer as well as to the office or workplace where that computer is located.

That, at least, is being tried by some Mexican associates of Aerotec, a multi-national company making a wide range of products, including digital imaging devices.

Jorge Luis Alvarado Cordova, a 5S coordinator for an Aerotec plant in Chihuahua, Mexico, says that the idea originally came from another Aerotec facility and was adapted at Chihuahua. His computer version of 5S is:

Sort. Take time to check all your files and software, and get rid of any that are unnecessary. The benefit: Faster processing time because more memory is available.

Simplify. Organize your files and optimize the use of file folders. Keep in mind how often you need them and how much time you need to store them. Create specific shortcut icons for the most used files or programs.

Sweep. Eliminate any files under deleted items, sent items and the recycle bin.

Standardize. Establish procedures for maintaining your computer 5S system. Involve the MIS department.

Self-discipline. Include this in 5S audits and focus on how people maintain files and program organization, and the time they spend doing so.

TAKEAWAYS

- 5S methods can be virtual as well as physical.
- Thinking of your hard drive as a place where files are stored is the right approach.
- Maintenance and audit procedures are important, and should involve the IT department.

12

Simple, Early Wins
Help Build Support
for Office Lean Efforts

March, 2004

Finding a way to save money on postage is a good idea, but it has little or nothing to do with lean production methods.

However, that kind of cost-saving measure can be a good way to get people started on a lean journey. Quick wins – actions that produce immediate benefits – help motivate people and build enthusiasm for improvement programs. They may then make it easier to get people involved in true lean initiatives, aimed at streamlining processes.

That has been part of the strategy recently as Siemens Business Services (SBS) in the United Kingdom seeks to transform National Savings and Investments (NS&I), a financial services operation previously run by the government.

Over the first six years of the effort, which began in January 2003, SBS expects the transformation will yield savings of £2.157 million, according to Willy Carroll, operations transformation manager.

It is an example of what increasingly is being called office lean, the application of lean principles to non-manufacturing operations. The stated goal is to take what had been a slow-moving bureaucracy with a history of failed, "flavor-of-the-month" improvement efforts and transform it into a self-managing, team-based culture with "an embedded continuous improvement environment."

Among the benefits emerging so far at NS&I's three sites are:

- A 65 percent reduction in internal travel equating to more than 450 man-hours per year.

- Elimination of certain reminders and forms saving 100 days annually.

- A savings of nearly 75 percent in certain manual work.

Improvements in Stages

NS&I sells bonds, certificates and savings accounts to consumers. Under a £1 billion contract of at least 10 and possibly 15 years, SBS is now managing all operational, administrative and IT services for NS&I.

The organization oversees investments of £60 billion in 63 million accounts for 30 million customers. SBS describes NS&I as having been plagued by "legacy systems and ways of working" and "high reliance on manual clerical operations."

The improvement effort got under way in September 2002 when Siemens hired the Bourton Group consulting firm to help. Over the next few months, senior managers were trained, a steering committee was appointed, pilot training began at the three sites and facilitators were selected. Benefits from the pilot efforts were reviewed in December, and a year-long, full-scale rollout began in January 2003.

NS&I had also been engaged in what Carroll describes as "an aggressive IT development program," which he concedes "probably didn't deliver to the extent expected. As a consequence, we've already done process improvements. We needed something that engaged people."

Some of the first improvements have been simple ways to save money. For example, one pilot effort found that using first-class postage was unnecessary, and that by switching to second-class postage, the area covered by the pilot project could save £2000 per year. By applying that philosophy to all operations, the savings grew to £94,000 per year.

More savings were found in practices related to passbook accounts. Many consumers regularly mail their bank books to NS&I to have the interest posted. Many include stamped, self-addressed envelopes for the return of the books. Those are not used (because NS&I achieves savings by returning the books through its own mass mailings), and the stamped envelopes were being thrown out. However, an improvement team discovered that NS&I could receive payment for returning the unused stamps to the post office – to the tune of £18,000 annually.

However, it is from true process improvements through applying lean principles that executives expect to achieve the greatest savings as well as increases in capacity. For example, one early effort targeted the processes involved in handling consumer orders for a particular bond product. Orders are received in the mail, data must be entered into the computer and typically six days elapsed from receipt of the application to getting everything out the door.

A team set a target of reducing that time period to four days. But with value stream mapping and application of lean methods, it actually brought the process down to three days.

"A lot of it has to do with double handlings and re-batching," Carroll notes. "A batch would sit until we had 50. By reshaping the process, we eliminated a lot of this sitting and doing nothing."

Already, improvements have freed up about 1,000 square meters of office space, Carroll says. While some processes now require less manpower, no one has been laid off because of the efforts. "We are looking for redeployment opportunities," he adds.

Equally important is the cultural change. There was skepticism early on Carroll says, because "we'd been through multiple initiatives, especially as part of government service. It was the flavor of the month – what was popular with whatever minister was in power at the time. But there was no real commitment from the top. One difference we're finding here is that the managers that come into this from Siemens have been very committed."

As with any lean transformation, support and momentum snowballed "once we got a critical mass going," says Carroll.

Today he is a full-fledged convert, a true believer who constantly thinks in lean terms. "At any other organization I look at, I think 'I could work miracles,'" he states.

TAKEAWAYS

- Non-lean improvements can build buy-in if they are perceived as part of a lean initiative.
- Mapping processes identifies waste, such as duplicate handlings of paperwork.
- Early success can build support from top management.

13

Tips for White Collar Kaizens

March, 2000

At some point after you begin a lean transformation of the shop floor, you'll look at a white-collar area and think, Hmmm, I wonder if ...

The answer is, Yes. Lean and TPM principles apply to white-collar areas as well as the shop floor.

A good example is Bundy North America, an $800-million unit of U.K.-based TI Group Plc that makes fluid carrying systems for automotive and refrigeration applications with 40 plants and offices and 7,000 employees. In 1997, it launched a lean conversion effort, called "common sense manufacturing" in its plants, according to James Davis, president, of parent TI Group Automotive Systems.

"We got some very quick results," he recalled during a presentation at a Productivity Inc. Best of North America Conference on lean production. For instance, inventory levels came down by 25 percent in a few months. "The problem was that the office didn't necessarily relate to common sense manufacturing," said Davis.

So, Bundy began a drive at its Michigan headquarters to apply lean in an effort called "common sense administration." Davis quipped that the term is as incongruous as "government intelligence" or "jumbo shrimp." Nevertheless, Bundy began applying lean business practices and principles in administrative and commercial areas.

Kaizen Focus	Before	After	Actions
Quote preparation	14 steps, 1-2 week lead time, 7% on-time, 40% reworked	11 steps, 1-2 days lead time, 83+% on-time, errors caught	Work cell created with desks to improve communication and quality
Office inventory	Multiple storage locations, 52 boxes of paper, 31 of transparencies, weekly deliveries	2 boxes of commonly used paper, 9 of transparencies, daily deliveries	Office supplies kept in one location, kanban cards trigger daily deliveries
Video conferencing	2-3 hours MIS help needed, pre-planning, confusing procedures, seldom used	No MIS help, no pre-planning, used more often	Manual reduced to one page of instructions, cable connections color coded

Getting started in office areas turned out to have similarities with launching lean in a plant. People wanted a "secret formula" for improvement, but, of course, there is none, Davis noted. Implementation is a matter or learning and applying the principles.

But to speed up the effort, Bundy added "a bit of a catalyst," according to Davis. The company hired Jim Thompson, author of *The Lean Office: How to Use Just-in-Time Techniques to Streamline Your Office* (1997 Productive Publications, Toronto). "We read it and liked it," said Davis. Thompson studied the Toyota Production System, the original lean system, while on a two-year assignment from GM to NUMMI, GM's joint venture with Toyota in Fremont, Calif. While there he began applying lean techniques and principles to the office.

Practical Advice

Thompson ran in-house seminars at Bundy headquarters on a level that "people could relate to," said Davis, who closed each seminar stressing the need for all to get involved and do one improvement project a month. Like the effort in the plant, the emphasis was put on action to avoid paralysis by over-analysis. Thompson offers these practical ideas for implementing lean in an office:

- Start with muda (waste.) Teach people that the starting point for action is the identification and elimination of the seven kinds of waste (Lean Manufacturing Advisor, Feb. 2000). Bundy added an eighth one for wasting talent. This helps them understand the goal of lean: maximize profits by lowering costs through the total elimination of waste. Implementing lean then becomes a progression of moving from a general principle (eliminating the waste of inventory) to finding the specific example in your office (excess amounts of copy paper.) This gives people a road map to follow. "Unless you have it, you won't know where you are going or when you are lost," said Thompson. From waste, move on to other key concepts such as standardized work and 5S.

- Next, launch monthly office kaizen projects to identify and eliminate the waste. Maintain the momentum of the kaizen effort by figuring out specifically for your culture what you should recognize and reward. Put your energy where it will do the most good – skip keeping count of how many kaizens you run in favor of making the improvement ideas visible by sharing them on bulletin boards or an intranet. Setting aside time during staff meeting agendas to recognize people for improvement ideas is another good way to share ideas and build involvement

- Executives are not exempt from kaizens. "Is the program just for the little people?" asked Thompson. "Everybody plays, that's leadership."

- Inspect to see if you taught the concepts effectively. Do people really understand waste, 5S and standardized work? The way you inspect is to walk around and ask people questions about what they are doing.

To drive the office effort, Bundy held informal kaizen reporting sessions every eight to 10 weeks. Each support function had to describe some of the improvements it had implemented. "This was primarily to force accountability, but the great part was sharing successes so people could learn from it," explained Davis.

One unit created a simple chart with months across the top and people's names down the left. When people did their monthly kaizen, they wrote it on a 3" x 5" index card and posted it on the chart in the proper month. This simple visual control made the monthly kiaizen target self-managing while adding a bit of peer pressure.

But the company also wanted the effort to be fun so it came up with the in-house slogan of RIDE the COMET to identify eight types of waste:

Rework
Inventory
Delay

Conveyance
Overproduction
Motion
Extra processing steps
Talent.

The company also created t-shirts and mouse pads with the slogan. In the cafeteria, it placed a board to display some of the best improvement ideas in between the normal reporting sessions of eight or 10 weeks. Ideas were shared over the company intranet, too.

Here are examples of the kaizens implemented in office areas:

Quicker Quotes

People in an area that prepared business quotes for a main customer mapped the process and took out three steps from the 14-step procedure. A process that used to take one to two weeks, now took one to two days. People who worked on the quotes were seated throughout the office, which consumed time when someone went looking for a co-worker.

Team members created the equivalent of a work cell by moving their desks together. "It did a great job in terms of improving communication," said Davis. Separate file cabinets in five different locations were consolidated into four within the "cell."

Employee also cross-trained each other so they could help fellow team members wherever a constraint developed in the quote process. Before this kaizen, 40 percent of quotes required rework. Today, problems are caught and fixed during processing. In five months, the number of quotes prepared on-time went from 7 percent to 83 percent and higher.

Saving $$$

General offices supplies were kept in various locations throughout the building. With 250 people in the corporate office "we had 250 storage areas," said Davis. "Everybody had their own stash in a drawer." Now there is a common storage location near receiving. It is screened off but not locked to send a message of trust.

A secretary championed a team to eliminate excess inventories of office supplies. "We were doing some very foolish things," said Davis. For instance, there were 52 boxes of 5 types of copy paper.

All the paper in storage was removed. Two boxes of the two most common types are kept in inventory. Two or three packages of paper are kept at each copy machine. The last package has a kanban ticket. When the package is opened, the ticket is pulled and placed in a reorder area where the supplier picks them up.

Paper, which had been ordered once a week through requisitions, now is delivered daily, based on the kanbans. The paper supplier already was making daily stops to deliver other items. The next step is to scan or transmit the order live and get replenishment the same day, which would allow company to take inventory down even further.

Other improvements included reducing inventory of 31 boxes of five different types of transparencies to nine boxes of just three types So far, the effort has reduced inventory of office supplies, by "multi-thousands of dollars," Davis estimated.

Executive Kaizens

Video conferencing had been "very, very difficult to do," said Davis, who took on the task of improving the process as a kaizen. Establishing a connection with another office required planning, scheduling, and two to three hours of help from MIS. Now, users need no assistance. The thick user's manual was boiled down to a simple, one-page, double-spaced laminated form of operating instructions and features. All cables and connectors are color-coded for easy checking. "Anybody can come in and use it in five minutes," said Davis.

Davis wasn't the only executive involved in office kaizens. The vice president of operations, who is responsible for 25 plants, did a kaizen on a fax machine.

"You might think, Why is he wasting his time on that?" said Davis. But when the office staff went home around 5 p.m. Davis and the vice president discovered that "between us we can't operate a fax machine."

The vice president developed simple instructions and a color-code scheme for local, long distance, and international calls. The system is being used on other office fax machines, too.

"There always is a simpler, better way," said Thompson. The same principles apply as in production. And the result is the same –

lower costs. "But it's also a great motivator," said Davis. "It reduces stress and makes work more enjoyable."

TAKEAWAYS

- Lay the foundation for office kaizens by teaching employees about identifying waste.
- High-level executive offices are not exempt from improvement efforts.
- Conduct projects monthly and hold informal reporting sessions every eight to 10 weeks to sustain the effort.

14

Invoicing and Receiving Receive the Kaizen Treatment

By Anthony Perna

July, 2000

While working for a mid-sized manufacturer of pneumatic components and systems, I had the opportunity to take part in, as well as facilitate, many kaizen events. Kaizen was a key component to our lean manufacturing efforts and continues to return many gains in productivity, space utilization, and inventory reduction.

Having already completed kaizen events in the more traditional areas of assembly and machining, we solicited input from managers in accounting, purchasing, shipping, receiving, information technology, and customer service. We found overlap among these service areas in receiving goods from suppliers and invoicing them. The result was a very cumbersome and time-consuming process.

We decided to kaizen the receiving and invoicing process. This event illustrated that improvement isn't restricted to manufacturing, nor does it have to be new or cutting-edge. Dramatic improvements can be right there for the taking. Here is what we did:

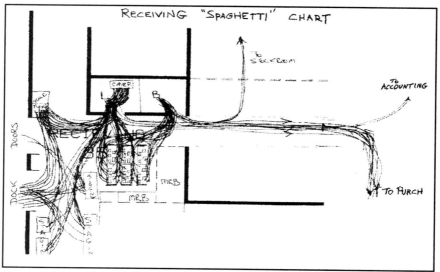

The receiving area "spaghetti diagram" before the kaizen event. The total walking distance was 10,688 feet to process incoming parts from vendors.

Conditions

The scope of this kaizen event was to streamline the receiving process from goods arrival at the dock to the point of payment to the supplier. We had been pursuing lean as a formalized practice for about 18 months at this point. We started with the operations side of the business, focusing on manufacturing (machining, turning, molding), assembly, and administration, then started to look at supporting functions. Our philosophy was to cover all areas which effected the customer, not just manufacturing. This led us to the receiving kaizen.

The easiest way to describe the current process was to flow chart it. For this article, I have included only significant steps. Still, the amount of nonvalue-added and wasteful activity is apparent.

We set the boundary conditions of this process to begin with the Receiving Department dropping off the prior days receiving paperwork at the Purchasing Department. It ends with the Accounts Payable clerk releasing payment to the supplier. The process shown is absent of any defective materials received, discrepancies in paperwork, or early shipment decision branches.

Process Steps

Walk to purchasing to deliver yesterday's receiving documents →
pick up new orders and walk back to receiving → place orders in
paper filing system → truck delivery arrives → driver drops off
delivery paperwork and unloads truck onto receiving dock →
move received material to staging area → walk back to receiving
office → walk back to material to retrieve packing slips → return
to office → look up order in MRP system → find due date and
quantity → if early or over/under shipped, set pack slip in hold
file for future disposition → if received material as specified, pull
a copy of the purchase order (PO) from paper file → write date
and quantity received on purchase order → enter information
into MRP system → write down system generated receipt number on PO → walk to copier and make 3 copies → attach first
copy to pack slip and file in "complete" file → walk to staging
area → attach second copy to material → walk to purchasing
department → give third copy to buyer in charge of material →
walk back to receiving area → buyer approves and signs copy
and puts in receiver's mail box → later in day receiver walks back
to purchasing and picks up signed copy → walk back to receiving → receive material into system → quality assurance (QA)
tags material → QA looks up item in database → if inspection
needed, pull print and inspect → take approved paperwork to
accounting dept. → payables clerk pulls paper copy in accounting filing system → accounts payable (AP) matches paperwork
→ enters info into MRP AP system → staples copies together
and places in paper filing system to cut check for payment → at
pre-determined interval pull paper documents and cuts check.

Each department — purchasing, receiving, and accounting — had
its own filing system with redundant copies. All three people had to
write down information which was then entered into the system,
creating redundancy and the opportunity for error. We received all
raw materials, purchased component inventories, and expensed
items throughout the day, every day with this procedure.

This is a good time to note that the receiving dock is at the opposite end of the facility to the purchasing department and the accounting offices are on a second level. In summary we identified approximately 50 process steps, 43 of which were identified as waste. We measured a walking distance of 10,688 feet. Clearly there was room for significant improvement.

The Kaizen Event

Our kaizen events can range from one day to two weeks in length. We were very careful to select goals and objectives that fit the time allotted. Kaizen events can generate positive and enthusiastic results if there is a sense of accomplishment and challenge. Setting goals too low can result in a "so what" attitude. Setting goals too high with no chance for completion or closure can leave all of the participants with a sense of frustration.

We were running two shifts Monday through Friday at the time, and a three-day event seemed to accommodate participants from both shifts with minimal disruption to the business and to people's personal schedules. This duration fit our environment. I have worked with companies where two-day events and four-day events were the norm. Do what works best for your own unique situation.

This is the agenda we followed for the receiving kaizen. We followed similar agendas for most of our other events as well:

Kaizen Event Agenda

Day I

Training
Problem identification selected by the team
Setting of goals and objectives selected by the team

Day 2

Value stream/process mapping
Statement of current process
Brainstorming session to generate improvement ideas
Action list
Prioritize, sort, and start implementation

Day 3

Finish implementation
Verification of receivables through each department
Outstanding "to-do" list including due dates and responsible parties
Document/flow chart new process and procedure
Report out presentation to senior staff

The general area of improvement was selected from the list generated by management. We then solicited voluntary participation but also had to ensure we had the necessary skills and knowledge base covered. This was not a problem since there was a very dedicated and conscientious work force with a good mix of newer and senior workers.

The team consisted of representatives from quality, IT, accounting, finance, purchasing, receiving, and material handling. We scheduled a three-day event, but found that the magnitude of this process warranted a second three-day event to finish the Accounts Payables side. We held this second event two weeks later. This gave us time to finish any outstanding action items from the first event.

Each event followed the same basic format: we kicked off with a half-day of basic kaizen training. As a team, we selected the goals and objectives that we would accomplish in the time allotted. That took us to the end of the first day. Before leaving, we discussed the agenda for the following day.

Day Two started by breaking up the team into smaller sub-teams, each assigned to a specific area to document current practices. We tried to team up someone from each pertinent area with someone from a different area who would bring a "fresh set of eyes" to view the process.

The teams "mapped" out their part of the processes noting the total number of steps involved from receiving the part to paying the supplier. Distance traveled for people, paper, and parts was documented via "spaghetti charts." Space requirements were noted, and overall major time elements recorded.

Wasted Movement

It became apparent that the most severe form of waste in this process was the travel time of the people in the three main departments of purchasing, receiving, and accounts payable. The amount of paper, copies, and recording of redundant information was a close second. The teams now directed their focus on eliminating any waste associated with unnecessary motion and travel. With the aid of many self-adhesive notes, the final process map was constructed to show a clear picture from start to finish.

Next, the group got together for a brainstorming session to come up with ways to eliminate travel and unnecessary steps. The action list was assigned to individuals and sub-teams who were responsible for implementing the improvements, updating procedures, and scheduling times to train other employees.

During the brainstorming session the representative from the IT department mentioned that our MRP software had a three-way matching feature for purchase orders. Nobody used it or knew much about it.

The matching function allows a purchase order to be matched with a receiving transaction and then matched to the supplier invoice in accounts payables all electronically and available on-line. This revelation brought a long day two to a close. Again, we set the agenda for the next day before leaving.

Implementing

Day Three was a more physical day. The receiving dock area was a filthy, cluttered mess so the team applied the 5Ss to organize the area. Team members removed old racks, and painted walls, signs and floor markings.

They even organized the receiving person's desk and office area. Please note that the receiving person was part of this team and was involved in all the 5S efforts.

Other actions taken by the team included: locating a printer in the receiving office, turning on the three-way match functionality of the MRP system, eliminating paper copies of POs and packing slips, and documenting the new procedure. Also, QA began an effort to certify more suppliers with dock-to-stock status to reduce the need for incoming inspection.

New Improved Process

Truck delivery arrives → third party truck driver drops off delivery paperwork and unloads truck onto receiving dock → receiving person takes packing slip to office and calls up order on-line → verify due date and quantities → enters amounts directly into MRP system → receiving moves parts to point-of-use inventory location assigned and created by the kaizen team → AR runs daily items received report → cuts check to supplier.

Walking has been virtually eliminated. Any issues at receiving can be resolved by picking up the phone and calling purchasing or accounting. Photocopying and redundant paper files have been eliminated. Re-entering the same information has been eliminated. Real-time information is now available to all departments. Supplier problems such as over/under shipments and quality issues are resolved on the spot instead of days later.

Finally, each person in his or her respective department was given the authority, responsibility, and accountability to perform their jobs in an efficient and effective way.

This is one example of a continuous improvement solution that was right under our noses. By no means do I intend to make this look like a simple and obvious course of events. As anyone who has been through a kaizen event or process change endeavor knows, it is anything but simple. We have learned through trial and error that if you stay focused and avoid the temptation of short cuts, long-term positive gains will result. It never fails to amaze me how much can be accomplished in a few days when a group is focused and dedicated to a common objective.

The three-way match functionality has greatly simplified the receiving process and in return has made the parties involved more

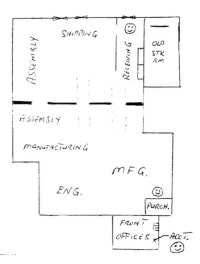

The kaizen team virtually eliminated walking between the receiving, accounting, and purchasing departments, shown here with smiling faces to reflect the improved process. Improvements included matching purchase orders electronically, removing clutter, and eliminating unnecessary steps. Receiving information is now available in real-time.

productive and their jobs less frustrating and burdensome. Because the actual owners of the process developed and implemented the ideas, there was overwhelming acceptance for this new procedure. Does your MRP system have this capability and if so, are you using it?

Anthony Perna now is vice president at an electrical heating manufacturer near Portland, Maine. With a background in engineering and manufacturing, he has worked for a number of companies implementing lean manufacturing.

TAKEAWAYS

- A standard process should be followed for all kaizen events.
- Even though offices are not engaged in physical labor, the greatest waste may lie in physical effort, such as walking between offices.
- Eliminating waste may involve coordinating the activities of different departments.

15

Delphi Lean Strategy Evolves to Go Beyond the Shop Floor

September, 2004

At some point in your lean journey, your efforts to become lean must extend beyond the shop floor to all other operations — finance, human resources, information technology, sales and marketing, product design and so on. That is the only way to truly become a lean enterprise and realize the full benefits of lean.

Making that happen is Robert Morgan's job. In the summer of 2004, Morgan stepped into the new position of executive-in-charge of lean business processes at Delphi, the global automotive supplier that employs more than 186,000 people worldwide.

"Bob's new assignment is particularly important for Delphi as we work to extend lean principles and practices across the entire company," says Donald Runkle, Delphi vice chairman and Morgan's boss. "While we have made good progress on deploying lean principles across our manufacturing operations and into our strategic suppliers, it's critical to additionally streamline our business processes to support Delphi's transformation into a truly lean enterprise."

The creation of Morgan's position represents an evolution of Delphi's approach as well as a subtle shift in strategy.

To date, all non-manufacturing areas "have been part of our wider lean enterprise initiative that has been keeping the organization informed of our steps," Morgan explains. "Within their own areas, they have been changing the way in which they do business to try and better support our change. What we have not done previously is to make the focus on those areas part of our policy deployment. Now it's an activity that says 'let's think about the whole activity of the support function.'"

Developing People

Morgan assumes his new role with a solid lean background. Most recently, he was director of lean operations for Delphi Thermal and Interior, and previously served as the manufacturing director for Delphi Harrison. His background also includes 15 years at TRW. Delphi describes him as an expert in lean principles, experienced in general management. He serves on the board of the Lean Enterprise Institute.

Delphi openly models its approach on the Toyota Production System, and Morgan comments, "The Toyota Way is not a shop floor way. It's actually a complete way of thinking about your business, your leadership, the way in which you develop people within your business."

Accordingly, Morgan's first efforts are focusing on developing people. He is beginning with what he describes as "very senior leadership" at the corporate level, people in each of the support functions, providing them with the training necessary to become lean leaders. The effort will then extend to top support people in Delphi's operating units.

"The type of development process that we will go through will first start at the gemba, the shop floor, in order to create the understanding of flow, the waste that exists within flow, the importance of standardization. Then we will be taking those principles and carrying them back to other process activities," Morgan explains.

(Gemba is a Japanese word that literally means "the real place." In manufacturing, it means the shop floor, where the actual product

92

is being made. A principle of lean manufacturing is to "go to the gemba.")

Delphi operates what it calls a "lean college" as well other lean leadership schools, and "we have put literally hundreds of people at the senior executive level through those training processes in the last four years," says Morgan. "Maybe 80 percent have been plant managers and from mainline manufacturing, while 20 percent have been from support functions. It's been somewhere between 300 and 400 executives worldwide. As we move into this initiative, that (proportion) will be reversed. We will be focused much more heavily in support. I think it's realistic to think that we will cover a similar number of executives and senior managers."

The Same Principles

The way that Morgan says Delphi plans to improve support departments is a classic lean approach: use of value stream mapping to understand current operations, creation of a future-state vision, the setting of specific goals, and implementation of improvement efforts to achieve those goals.

Gains from addressing the so-called low-hanging fruit — obvious duplications and other forms of easily-seen waste — are likely immediately, but "then we'll also expect a step-by-step change to the way in which work is done, equal to our vision," he notes. "Rather than just pruning, we've got a vision of what we want this to look like. Rather than just cut the top off, we're shaping to a particular form."

"Hard financial goals" will be given to the business-unit presidents, built into operating-unit budgets, and "they will be expected to deliver as a result of the way functional departments will change," he adds.

And Morgan believes the support departments can achieve the same degree of improvement that lean efforts yield on the shop floor. For example, he notes, "we are well over 99 percent for on-time delivery. Our premiums to achieve on-time delivery are at the lowest level they have ever been, and we are still achieving 50 percent improvements. We would expect to see the same thing in on-time delivery (in support areas), whether it is designs to customers, prototypes to customers or payroll to employees. The principles carry across.

"Whenever we go into an area, and it doesn't matter how good we are, we can get a 30-to-40-percent improvement in pure labor productivity. There's no reason to believe this group of people should have any more or less improvement opportunities than a group of people assembling an engine system."

Underlying all this is Delphi's belief — as well as Toyota's — that continuous improvement is all about people.

"One of the very early learnings Toyota teaches on the shop floor is 'respect the operator,'" Morgan notes. "It's a means of putting pride and customer focus into the work your employees do. That translates into every support department. An operator is not just a person on the shop floor. A supervisor is not just a person on the shop floor.

"It's time to look within our own houses. I'm really enthusiastic about what this can do, and it's significantly different from any other auto parts suppliers. I'm really excited.

TAKEAWAYS

- A lean transformation must include support processes.
- Training begins at the top.
- Percentage gains should match those on the shop floor.

16

Improving Flow in an Office Setting

June, 2001

Re-examining a value stream pays off, even if the initial improvements were substantial. Such a reassessment in a professional office operation at Rockwell Collins resulted in a complete rethinking of value, opening the way to even bigger improvements.

The re-examination, which began when the first pilot project was barely underway, is completely changing the process for producing technical manuals. "We're transforming from a publishing business to an information management solutions provider," said Scott Watson, senior director of technical operations. "In the lean transformation process, we're moving from mass production to mass customization."

In the initial phase of the lean transformation, writers, editors, and illustrators at the company's Aviation Services unit in Cedar Rapids, Iowa, were co-located into "cells," which cut the average time to publish manuals from five months to five weeks. But the follow-up re-examination of the value stream is generating changes that will allow information to be rapidly developed into a variety of paper and electronic formats that can be made into customized products for customers.

"Lean will eliminate waste and reduce costs, and that's great," said Watson, "but we're using lean to create expanded products and services at lower costs by freeing up capacity."

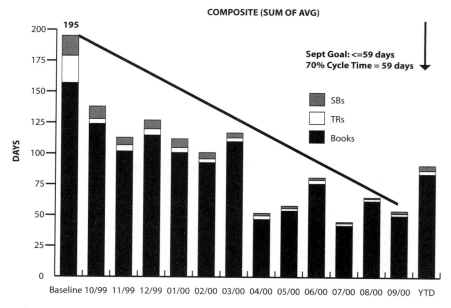

COMPOSITE (SUM OF AVG)

Sept Goal: <=59 days
70% Cycle Time = 59 days

- SBs
- TRs
- Books

DAYS

Baseline 10/99 11/99 12/99 01/00 02/00 03/00 04/00 05/00 06/00 07/00 08/00 09/00 YTD

MONTH

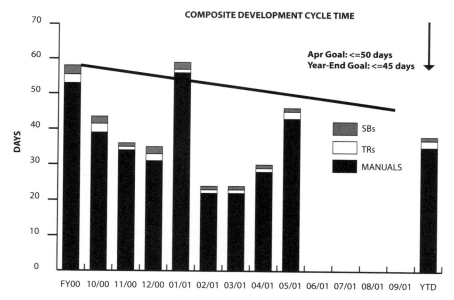

COMPOSITE DEVELOPMENT CYCLE TIME

Apr Goal: <=50 days
Year-End Goal: <=45 days

- SBs
- TRs
- MANUALS

DAYS

FY00 10/00 11/00 12/00 01/01 02/01 03/01 04/01 05/01 06/01 07/01 08/01 09/01 YTD

MONTH

The above charts are used at the Collins Aviation Services unit of Rockwell Collins to track the individual cycle times for producing three types of publications and the composite cycle time for producing all three. The two charts track improvement over a 20-month period. The time to produce service bulletins (SB) is represented by the gray band at the top of the bar and the band below represents temporary revisions. The bottom section, which is also the biggest band on the bar, represents books or technical manuals. Although titled a little differently, the charts track the some measure from last fiscal year to the current one. In January 2001, the average cycle time spiked up because a 12-day holiday shut down was counted in the measure. The reason for counting calendar days is that customers, which are the airlines, fly every day.

What ultimately became the lean journey began in 1999 when the senior management team "saw the need to provide greater value to our customers in our service environment," Watson recalled. Senior managers wanted the service business to shift from a product-centric to a customer or solution-centric focus. "By doing that we could re-invent ourselves and take another leap in the market," he said.

Batching Books

The technical publications unit within Collins Aviation Services produces and updates operation guides, maintenance manuals, training courses, installation manuals, illustrated parts catalogs, service bulletins, and service information letters for the "black boxes" or avionics that the company makes. The content and format of the publications must meet Federal Aviation Administration (FAA) and Air Transport Association (ATA) specifications. Since products change throughout their lifecycles, so must the documents supporting them.

As a result, temporary changes are made to manuals "constantly," said Watson. The temporary changes must become regular parts of revised manuals within time periods set by industry regulations. The result was continual revisions to production cycles to accommodate the changes. The process could easily "mushroom into a huge cloud of costs and wastes," said Watson. But the manuals are absolutely essential to aerospace customers trying to maintain and operate technical equipment at hundreds of locations worldwide. As the aerospace market consolidated, customers needed to update and manage their technical documentation faster and more efficiently.

The value stream serving these customers was segmented. Writers, illustrators, and editors worked in three buildings in separate functional departments, much like people and equipment in a plant set up for mass production would work in departments dedicated to welding, milling, or grinding. The result was poor communication and delays as work was handed off in batches from one process to the next, where it waited in queue.

"We looked at this and decided we had to streamline the flow," said Watson. The illustrators, editors, and writers were relocated into one building in 1999. "That was simply a reorganization decision," he recalled. "Now the real work began. Our challenge was to transform ourselves, and the perfect tool or as we like to call it, the change engine, was lean principles."

An ambitious goal of cutting publishing cycle times by 80 percent was added to the department's objectives and the review criteria for its 137 employees. A team of employees and supervisors, working with an outside consultant, mapped and analyzed the value stream and created a leaner one by configuring desks into a pilot cell staffed by a four-person team of illustrators, writers, and an editor.

Identifying Demand and Skills

Designing the cell or "bullpen" followed a process that will be familiar to anyone who has set up continuous flow cells on the shop floor, but with a few differences. One was that arranging workstations in processing sequence was not as critical as in a production cell. People sit along the inside perimeter of the cell's wall, close enough together to make communication easy. The wall is low to facilitate communication with others in the room. Another distinction is that "every job is a little bit different," said Gary Haberkorn, department director. "The products we put out are not really homogeneous." For instance, teams produce product updates as well as complete revisions. And formats differ from book to book. A different product means a different takt time. "To deal with this, we simply took our products to the lowest common denominator: a page. We use a page to figure takt time instead of a book."

Still, creating the pilot cell was "not a whole lot different" than creating one on the shop floor, said Kevin Henning, a consultant with Simpler Consulting, Inc. The implementation team had to determine what customer demand was, list the work elements and skills needed to produce a product, and balance the work among the people in the cell. "The toughest thing was determining what customer demand was," said Henning. Because of a work backlog, the team had to make a judgment call on how much work was new work and how much of the backlog it wanted to complete each month. This was translated into how many pages had to be produced annually, then how many had to be produced each month. This was divided by the available time to get a takt time, which is the rate of customer demand.

Team members identified the major skills needed to produce manuals — editing, illustrating, and writing — and the work elements within each. Any steps that were wasteful were eliminated to avoid moving them into the cell. Based on their experiences, team members were able to estimate how much time was needed to do each work element. This information was used to create a rough bar chart, to determine how to staff the cell.

The bar chart was similar to, but not as accurate as the operator balance chart used to staff a lean production cell. Still, it was a useful tool in the office environment. Each block within a vertical bar represented a work element and was proportional to the time needed to do the work. A horizontal line at the top of the chart indicated takt time – how many books had to be produced in a week. The sum of the time of the work elements was divided by the takt time to determine how many people were needed in a cell. The total work elements for each person in the cell should approach but not exceed the takt time.

Visual Controls

Work begins on a manual when the team receives the product data and engineering drawings. It holds a "kickoff meeting" for "a day or so" to study the material and analyze the best way to do the job, explained Haberkorn. For example, the team may decide that a writer can work on some text, while the editor checks the rest for proper formatting, while the illustrator puts drawings in the right format and order. When a section is done, it goes to the editor for checking.

Ideally, only one job should be in a cell at any time. However, when someone is within a day or two of finishing work on a project, he or she can request work from the next project, explained Henning. Two is the maximum number of books that the cell can have at any time.

Visual controls alert management if there is a problem or potential problem. A post outside of the cell holds colored flags. Purple indicates a potential work stoppage. Green means there is plenty of work. Yellow means another job will be needed in less than five days. Red means there is less than a day's worth of work. "If there is a work stoppage, the manager gets involved right away," said Haberkorn. Another visual display shows how many of the tasks needed to finish a book are completed.

Computerized indicators show jobs that are due within the next week, work-in-process, cost performance, and schedule performance. Key performance metrics, reviewed weekly, gauge cycle time, productivity, and quality. "But what our customers told us first and foremost," said Haberkorn, "is they care about on-time delivery." Customers also told them they had a different idea of what value was. Even as the initial improvements were being made to the pilot cell, the team looked at the value stream again, taking a deeper and broader perspective that included customers.

Re-defining Value

"What we thought was value was not of the greatest value to our customer," Watson recalled. "We thought our product, once the process was leaned out, was the value our customers were looking for. We found out that one product didn't satisfy the demand for value. One size didn't fit all."

The unit discovered that the distinct groups using the technical manuals, such as pilots, maintenance technicians and engineers, among others, really wanted publications customized to their distinct needs. Existing manuals contained information aimed at these groups, but it wasn't enough. Customers really wanted manuals and training materials customized for their jobs, and they wanted them in electronic as well as paper formats. The new challenge was to deliver greater value for customers by offering them customized manuals in the different formats, while reducing the time to create them and maintaining the Rockwell Collins reputation for reliability, explained Watson.

A key to customization was moving the creation of manuals in Standard Generalized Markup Language (SGML) to the beginning of the publishing process. SGML is a text and document formatting language used for large databases and multi-media projects, particularly for ones with intensive cross-referencing and indexing. It makes documents and other files platform-independent and portable between applications. HyperText Markup Language (HTML) is an application of SGML that uses code as tags to tell web browsers how to display text and graphics.

In the old process, the SGML version of manuals had been created near the end of the publishing process, after the printed version. If it were moved to the front, a cell could develop a core product that was ready for customization. A core SGML document could be used to create paper or searchable electronic manuals for different computer platforms.

"The goal was to create information that could be developed or repurposed quicker than anybody in the industry," explained Watson. "When the core SGML product is revised all products are concurrently revised."

Moving SGML's place in the production flow required editors and writers to be cross-trained in its use. "We're not 100 percent there, but most of our cell teams are capable of writing in SGML," said Watson.

Change Management
Workplace changes such as learning new skills and new jobs required a substantial amount of change management. "Frankly there was resistance to all that change," Watson recalled. "We had

expeditors; we had schedulers. Our goal was to eliminate those functions, not those people. But that was pretty hard for any employee who had been expediting and scheduling for 10 years to swallow."

Transforming any organization is a change management challenge, according to Watson. That doesn't mean people don't want to change or work hard. It means they want to understand the new environment, the new tools, the new process, and how they fit in. "Everything is out of their comfort zone; it's all new to them," said Haberkorn.

Management led the process of creating the pilot cell and then replicating it by setting the direction and "boundary conditions" within which employees worked together to create the new cells. People drew current and future state maps and served on the kaizen teams that implemented the future state maps.

The office kaizens, called radical process improvement, began with a planning meeting four to six weeks before the event to define the scope and goals. The planning process could include meetings between teams, managers, and kaizen facilitators. A "magna carta" was drafted for the event, setting the team's responsibilities. For example, teams usually could spend between $5,000 and $10,000 before getting management approval. They could not fire people, but could move people and change their responsibilities. Haberkorn checked in daily with a kaizen team to see if additional support was needed. After four long days of work, a kaizen team reports to the management leadership team on what it had implemented.

Initially, kaizen teams examined the writing and illustrating processes to determine standard work, Haberkorn recalled. That set the stage for a kaizen team to create a team of illustrator, writer, and editor around a product line for the pilot cell. The kaizen team analyzed the work, broke it down into its elements, balanced the work among cell team members, and established a lean work flow based on standard work. By the end of the kaizen, people had been relocated to a cell. The first cell was operated and improved for six months before the practice of replicating it throughout the unit began.

At first, there was a "lot of disbelief that lean tools such as takt time would work or were needed, since the company was successful," said Watson. But as people participated in the kaizen process, working with customers and talking to them, they realized they could improve existing products and create new ones. And they realized first-hand how they were adding value. The time needed to produce a manual dropped from nine months to one.

To help support the transition to the new lean system, the company made training videos that included testimonials from people who were enjoying the increased responsibility and empowerment of the cell team configuration. Selected people are recognized monthly by the company and fellow employees. Teams have daily meetings called "huddles," and get email broadcasts about what customers are saying – good and bad. If a team misses an objective, it performs a root cause analysis to fix the problem. For instance, teams report the number of pages completed each week. If it is below the goal, they do an analysis to understand why.

Tips

That type of thoroughness plays a key role in the success of applying lean principles in a professional office environment, just as it does on the shop floor, Henning said. Another tip to adopt from the Rockwell Collins experience is to draw a current state map of the office value stream, then ask yourself what does your organization have to do to separate itself from the competition. "Have that goal in mind for your future state," he said.

The future state map helps you to see where to hold kaizen events so they improve an entire value stream, instead of isolated processes in it. "Lots of times people do kaizen just because someone said they should and not with a clear idea of how to measure improvement or what they expect to get out of it. So they do events that help a little bit here and there, but don't link together to produce a dramatic end result," Henning said. Finally, revisit the value stream multiple times to continue making improvements. "That's one of the toughest things in any environment," said Henning. People do one kaizen and think, "Everything's fixed and now we'll stay like this forever."

TAKEAWAYS

- A second effort to improve a value stream can produce as much or more improvement as the first.
- One-piece flow can be implemented by making sure an office cell only works on one project at a time.
- Training and change management are just as critical in offices as in manufacturing.

17

Spreadsheets and Data Are Tools in Quest for the Lean Office

August, 2003

Some people identify waste by drawing value stream maps on large pieces of paper or on whiteboards. Jose Zavala uses spreadsheets.

Zavala holds the title of APQP (advance product quality planning)/quality engineering manager at Delphi's Packard Electric plant in Los Mochis, Mexico. He targets waste in non-manufacturing processes. In 1997, he developed a solution for handling documentation for the product parts approval process and created a related Microsoft Excel-based application that is now used in many locations.

His current efforts involve a spreadsheet program used to help target lean office initiatives — a method he outlined during a presentation at the 2003 Shingo Prize conference.

It's a detailed, data-intensive approach to rooting out waste, and Zavala believes it produces a number of benefits.

First, he explains, "it helps me to measure something that is very subjective. Measurement is the first requisite for improvement. If you don't know where you are, how can you improve?"

Second, "it's like a picture that you take of the current process. It gives you the insight, the details of the current state and helps you pinpoint areas of opportunity."

Also, "it helps me be more systematic. I have a methodology, which is the way I can see it right or wrong. It helps me be consistent."

And finally, Zavala says, "it provides the lingo. It helps me to speak the same language with all the people involved. It drives commonalities."

Identifying Value

Zavala's spreadsheet approach creates a map of office processes. In Figure 1 — the macro part of the spreadsheet — each box shows a step in the process of how a company purchases a personal computer (PC). The letter in the upper right of each box (A, B, C, etc.) identifies the person performing that task.

Once the steps are identified and laid out in sequence, a team working on the initiative estimates three numbers for how long that step takes: the most optimistic completion time, the most likely time and the most pessimistic time, measured in days. (Zavala

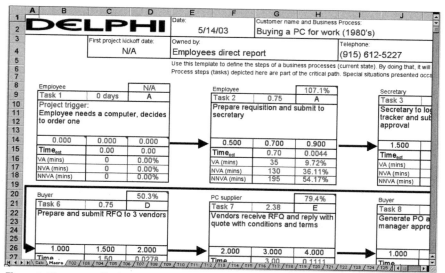

Figure 1. The macro display of a Delphi lean map spreadsheet.

No	ACTIVITY description	Dist (yds)	Accum Dist	Time (mins)	Assum Time	Staff	Accum Staff	OPER
1	Requests catalog to secretary (phone)	0	0	5	5	1	1	+
2	Delay until secretary has catalog available	0	0	45	50	0	1	
3	Obtains catalog	30	30	5	55	1	2	
4	Selects a particular model from catalog	0	30	60	115	1	3	0
5	Research other sources (phone)	0	30	120	235	1	4	0
6	Make final decision for PC model	0	30	30	265	1	5	+
7	Asks for a requisition form	0	30	5	270	1	6	0
8	Wait for requisition form to be available	0	30	30	300	0	6	
9	Gets blank requisition form	50	80	5	305	1	7	

DELPHI

Customer name and Business Process: Buying a PC for work (1980's)
Size of the project (example: number of components per prototype order, marketing address, etc): 1 PC, standard size and capacity, any brand
Task 2: Prepare requisition and submit to secretary
Primary system outcome: Desktop PC available in the market
Owned by: Employees direct report
By: Employee
Telephone: (915) 612-6
FROM MACRO: 0.5 Optim 0.5 Most L 0.7

Figure 2. Time observations of each step in a process.

defines completion time as the period from the point at which all inputs are provided to the next process, to the point in time at which the process generates all the expected outputs.) These are displayed in the horizontal boxes across the middle of each box. For example, in the second box — Task 2, Prepare requisition and submit to secretary — the most optimistic time is 0.5 days, the most likely 0.7 days and the most pessimistic 0.9 days.

Then the time required for each step is actually measured — by someone other than the operator — and the observations are recorded, as shown in Figure 2, which displays the results of observations made just for Task 2. A critical part of this process is that each activity is classified, in two ways. First, it is classified as to the type of activity: operation, transportation, inspection or storage, and is marked under the appropriate column, also in Figure 2. Second, it is classified as to its value; A plus sign (+) in the column means the activity is value-adding (VA). A minus sign (-) is non-value-adding (NVA). A zero (0) denotes activity that is necessary but non-value-adding (NNVA).

These observations are summarized in the Conclusion section, shown at the top of the next page. In this case, the most likely estimated time (0.7 days, which translates into 336 minutes) turned into an actual observation time of 360 minutes. This amount is divided up into the value-adding and non-value-adding amounts shown in both minutes and percentages. These numbers are also

Estimated Mins	Conclusion			Total
336				360
Var in Mins	VA (+)	NVA (-)	NNVA (0)	
2.1	35	130	195	
arlance	% on detailed t	% VA	% NVA	% NNVA
.004	107.1%	9.72%	36.11%	54.17%

transferred into the lower part of the box for this step in the macro display (Figure 1). In this case, only 35 minutes of the total 360 minutes, or 9.72 percent, is value-adding.

Also in the box for this step in Figure 1: The 360 minutes is expressed as 0.75 days, along the top line. At the very top right of the box, the 360 minutes translates into 107.1 percent of the time originally estimated.

In the middle of the box, on the line labeled Time, 0.70 (days) is the average expected time for each task to take place (under regular circumstances). This is calculated by applying the formula

$$t_e = (o + 4*m + p) / 6$$

where [o] is the Optimistic time, [m] is the Most likely time and [p] is the Pessimistic time. 0.0044 corresponds to the degree of uncertainty (where zero represents consistency or predictability). It is calculated with the formula:

$$\sigma2 = [(p - o) / 6]2$$

using the same variables as on the previous calculation.

Spotting Anomalies

The true benefit of this approach comes when all the data for steps in a process are summarized, as shown in Figure 3. This shows the total value-adding time, and how much time is spent on the process by each person involved.

But it is the three bar charts, shown in Figure 4 that provide the

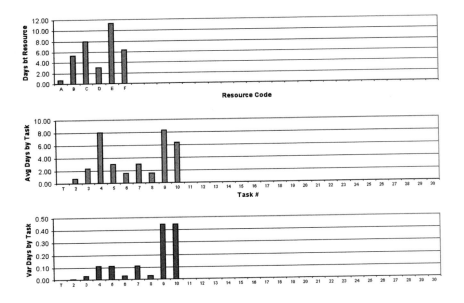

	Code	Name and / or title	Accumulated Time	Notes
9				
10	A	Employee	0.7000	
11	B	Secretary	5.3433	
12	C	Supervisor or Manager	8.0000	
13	D	Buyer	3.0000	
14	E	PC supplier	11.3333	Highest content
15	F	IS&S department	6.3333	

Figure 3. Summaries of time observations.

Figure 4. Identifying opportunities for improvement.

109

real insights into where the opportunities for improvement exist. The top one, Days by Resource, may identify someone who is not doing a proportional share of work (A), or a bottleneck (E). The second chart, Days by Task, may show how work needs to be leveled, or where a task is a bottleneck. The third chart, Variance in Days by Task, may raise questions about why a particular task has greater variance than others.

The approach produces real benefits, Zavala says. One example occurred when a team focused on the processes involved in confirming compliance with federal rules for certain products. (These include temperature tests, vibration tests, and so on.) The waste identified through Zavala's approach enabled the team to reduce the time for the processes from 80 days to 28.

Zavala stresses the need to focus on standardization of work practices and on achieving consistency. His advice to others is "Don't go for the home run."

But he also advises persistence. His philosophy: "If it ain't broke, keep looking!"

TAKEAWAYS

- Spreadsheets can help identify how long the steps in a process take, and how much of the time is value-added.
- Charts based on spreadsheet data can identify bottlenecks.
- Excessive variance can also be identified through this approach.

18

Publisher Makes Key Concepts a Daily Part of Its Newspapers

March, 2004

The editor of *The Record* daily newspaper, based in Hackensack, N.J., recently requested money to purchase laptop computers for reporters. As required by company policy, he presented current and future state process maps along with his request. The proposal is moving forward, partly because the maps showed giving reporters laptops would free up 70 man-hours per week.

Requiring that process maps accompany all capital requests is one example of how North Jersey Media Group, *The Record's* parent company, is integrating lean principles into daily decision-making. Process maps must also accompany all new-hire requests to show what benefit will be gained from adding a position.

North Jersey Media is not a manufacturer, unless you consider the printing of newspapers to be manufacturing. The company publishes two dailies plus 34 weeklies, and it posts news and information on the Web.

But as with growing numbers of manufacturers, its top management has launched the company on a lean journey and is involving every department in the transformation. The goal is to make continuous improvement an essential part of daily operations and the standard mindset for all employees.

Where's the Waste? You Only Have to Ask

It's not hard to get employees of a company to tell you what's wrong.

At a recent continuous improvement training session at *The Record* newspaper in Hackensack, N.J., instructor Mitchell Krugel taught those attending about different forms of waste, then asked them to come up with examples.

A pressroom worker talked about bad printing plates that never should have been put on the press. One worker described how a lack of space forced the company to move fully loaded pallets out of the main building to another location, then bring them back when the materials they held were needed. Several people complained about the time spent waiting for computers to boot up or simply to function. An employee criticized the "over-designed" voicemail system (he wasn't the first to do so). And an editor vented about the need to fix style problems in copy because the reporters who wrote the stories weren't familiar with the paper's stylebook. (However, he also admitted that the stylebook is in need of updating.)

Krugel says that, based on forms students fill out once the course is completed, he believes about 20 to 25 percent of them truly grasp continuous improvement concepts and want to apply them to broad company problems. Another 20 to 25 percent, he says, think in individual terms; they talk about value stream mapping their own day or applying 5S concepts to their own workspace.

"And we are also getting people who can't figure it out," he notes.

The result, executives hope, is to increase capacity. Mitchell Krugel, a full-time continuous improvement leader, says one example might be using more "press windows" (unused time on printing presses) to add editions or advertising inserts. "We probably won't be adding a lot of people, but we feel we can find the capacity for expansion, and more muscle for departments that need it," he says. "If we can find the crews, and people to write stories and edit and move papers out the door, that's where we need capacity."

The effort is still in its early stages. The first lean leaders were trained in 2003, and the brand new continuous improvement office was created at that time.

That office consists of three people: Krugel, who was formerly an editor in the sports department; Mike Ruiz, previously a pressroom supervisor; and Antoinette Senise, who still spends 40 percent of her time in human resources, where she had been working full-time. In addition, a dozen other employees have been trained as continuous improvement mentors, but they still work full-time in other departments.

While the current focus of the mentors is on training the workforce, some gains have already been achieved through lean initiatives:

- The percentage of pages that meet quality standards when they come off the press (and can therefore be distributed to readers) has jumped 40 percent.

- A continuous improvement team came up with ways to publish more color in the classified section, creating what Ruiz says is a half-million dollar revenue opportunity.

- Invoices to customers have been standardized, with the result that substantial "missing" revenue (meaning it wasn't properly accounted for) has now is being "found."

Training First

With much of their revenue from advertising, newspapers are sensitive to business cycles — and North Jersey Media is no exception. The "bottom started to drop out of the advertising market" about two years ago, Krugel notes.

As a result, company president Jon Markey, who was familiar with the elements of continuous improvement, began a push for their implementation to maintain profitability.

Each department has developed a policy and objectives (P/O) matrix, which is an x-type matrix used for strategic planning and which shows (on one sheet of paper) policies, objectives, metrics, who is responsible, the impact on the organization and the relationship between each of these factors.

Consultants from Productivity, Inc. trained the continuous improvement mentors. They, in turn, are now conducting day-long "CI 101" courses, each with about 30 students. Any worker can sign up for any class, with the result that any given class contains people from a wide range of departments.

After completing a class, each student fills out a feedback form. Its primary focus is how the student might apply what was learned to actual operations.

The initial focus is on providing basic training to all employees in the company's daily newspaper division, which accounts for two-thirds of the 1,800 employees. One of the next phases involves instruction for middle managers on how to manage CI opportunities.

There are also plans to develop a recognition and reward program and a continuous improvement intranet has been launched. A CI in-house newsletter is being started, and stories may appear in the company's quarterly magazine.

Another goal for this year is for department heads to conduct kaizen events to achieve specific improvements.

The company believes the training is going well, and "now it's just getting an implementation path in place," Krugel says. "We asked them to actually use the tools to do some work, and they came up with some interesting results. They saw the value and the power of it. Jon (Markey) is doing so many things to drive this. It's just a matter of time and getting more structural pieces in place."

TAKEAWAYS

- Requiring use of lean methods can improve business decision-making on capital spending, hiring, etc.
- Having a full-time continuous improvement staff is valuable.
- Employees are often the best source of improvement ideas.

Citations

(All articles taken from the *Lean Manufacturing Advisor*)

Chapter 1: "New Toyota Center Seeking To Make Sales and Marketing Lean." August 2002: Volume 4, Number 3

Chapter 2: "Transforming a Service Firm." June 2003: Volume 5, Number 1

Chapter 3: "Revamping Design Process Increases Speed and Quality." November 2003: Volume 5, Number 6

Chapter 4: "Call Center's Transformation Produces Award for Service." October 2002: Volume 4, Number 5

Chapter 5: "New Restaurant Owner Sees His Future in a Lean Lunch." April 2004: Volume 5, Number 11

Chapter 6: "Ambulance Office Responds to Calls for Improvements." November 2002: Volume 4, Number 6

Chapter 7: "Whether Office or Factory, the Same Principles Apply." October 2003: Volume 5, Number 5

Chapter 8: "Neither Culture Nor Equipment Stops Postal Transformation." October 2003: Volume 5, Number 5

Chapter 9: "Builders Seek to Demolish Inefficiency." December 2002: Volume 4, Number 7

Chapter 10: "First Steps to Making Your Office Lean." March 2003: Volume 4, Number 10

Chapter 11: "5S Techniques Can Clean Up the Hard Drive of a Computer." May 2003: Volume 4, Number 12

Chapter 12: "Simple, Early Wins Help Build Support for Office Lean Efforts." March 2004: Volume 5, Number 10

Chapter 13: "Tips for White Collar Kaizens." March 2000: Volume 1, Number 10

Chapter 14: "Invoicing and Receiving Receive the Kaizen Treatment." July 2000: Volume 2, Number 2

Chapter 15: "Delphi Lean Strategy Evolves to Go Beyond the Shop Floor." September 2004: Volume 6, Number 4

Chapter 16: "Improving Flow in an Office Setting." June 2001: Volume 3, Number 1

Chapter 17: "Spreadsheets and Data Are Tools in Quest for the Lean Office." August 2003: Volume 5, Number 3

Chapter 18: "Publisher Makes Key Concepts a Daily Part of Its Newspapers." March 2004: Volume 5, Number 10

Index

Lean Manufacturing Advisor ...

Your Monthly, Independent Source for First-Hand, Current, and Practical Advice.

If the articles in this book are proving helpful, and you want to stay current on the latest trends and developments in lean implementation, then you should subscribe to *Lean Manufacturing Advisor*.

Lean Manufacturing Advisor's editorial team gives you the behind-the-scenes news and advice, and real-life, how-to-implement details from people on the same continuous improvement journey as you. Its in-depth coverage demonstrates how you can be an effective agent of change and lead management and front line employees in a successful lean transformation.

Each month *Lean Manufacturing Advisor* covers the latest developments in lean manufacturing with these unique features:

- Case studies, featuring successful real-life lean initiatives, provide a wealth of ideas to share with your team.

- The Q&A section addresses common technical questions.

- Editorials offer advice, analysis, and commentary on the latest developments in lean manufacturing.

- Photos, diagrams, and samples documents show you what other companies are doing.

When you subscribe to *Lean Manufacturing Advisor,* you join a community of experienced executives and managers who have successfully implemented lean in their organizations. You'll leverage their experience, benchmark your progress, avoid the pitfalls, and speed lean implementation.

Get the insider's view that you can't find on corporate websites or in trade magazines, subscribe to *Lean Manufacturing Advisor!*

To subscribe, visit our website: www.productivitypress.com, or call toll-free at 1-888-319-5852. For multiple subscriptions of 3 or more copies, contact us at ehanus@productivitypress.com.